Agency and Intentions in Language

Linguistics

Volumes published in this Brill Research Perspectives title are listed at *brill.com/rplis*

Agency and Intentions in Language

Edited by

Julie Goncharov and Hedde Zeijlstra

BRILL

LEIDEN | BOSTON

Library of Congress Control Number: 2023908341

Typeface for the Latin, Greek, and Cyrillic scripts: "Brill". See and download: brill.com/brill-typeface.

ISSN 2667-0682
ISBN 978-90-04-67978-8 (paperback)
ISBN 978-90-04-67981-8 (e-book)

Copyright 2023 by Julie Goncharov and Hedde Zeijlstra. Published by Koninklijke Brill NV, Leiden, The Netherlands.
Koninklijke Brill NV incorporates the imprints Brill, Brill Nijhoff, Brill Hotei, Brill Schöningh, Brill Fink, Brill mentis, Vandenhoeck & Ruprecht, Böhlau, V&R unipress and Wageningen Academic.
Koninklijke Brill NV reserves the right to protect this publication against unauthorized use. Requests for re-use and/or translations must be addressed to Koninklijke Brill NV via brill.com or copyright.com.

This book is printed on acid-free paper and produced in a sustainable manner.

Contents

Preface VII
Notes on Contributors IX

Agency in the English Way-Construction's Constraints 1
    Caterina Cacioli
    Abstract 1
    Keywords 1
1   Introduction 1
2   The Way-Construction 3
3   Attributing Agency 8
    3.1   *An Effect for Movement* 10
4   Corpus Research and Analysis 12
    4.1   *Method* 12
    4.2   *Results* 13
    4.3   *Discussion* 20
5   Conclusions 22

On Some Epistemic Access Effects 27
    Francesco Costantini
    Abstract 27
    Keywords 27
1   Introduction 27
2   Subjunctive Obviation 29
3   Obviation and *de se* Attitude Reports 30
4   Epistemic Access as Source of Obviation 37
5   Other Expected Outcomes 41
6   Alternative Analyses 44
7   Concluding Remarks 49

Two Semantic Paths to Unintentional Causation 54
    Ömer Demirok
    Abstract 54
    Keywords 54
1   Introduction 54
2   Background on Un-agentive Constructions 56
    2.1   *Background in Typological Research* 56
    2.2   *Background in Theoretical Research* 58

- 3 Syntactic Contrasts 63
  - 3.1 *The Syntactic Anatomy of the Oblique Causer Construction in Laz* 65
  - 3.2 *The Syntactic Anatomy of the Circumstantial Modal Construction in Laz* 68
  - 3.3 *Interim Discussion* 71
- 4 Interpretational Contrasts 74
  - 4.1 *The Asymmetry in the Polysemy Profiles* 74
  - 4.2 *The Asymmetry in What Role the Oblique NP Has* 78
  - 4.3 *The Asymmetry in Downward Entailing Environments* 79
  - 4.4 *Summary of the Interpretational Contrasts* 82
- 5 Summary of the Claims and Remaining Questions 82

Letting Structure Speak with Authority: Constraining Agents' Choices with French *laisser* 88

Marta Donazzan, Clémentine Raffy, Bridget Copley and Klaus von Heusinger

Abstract 88

Keywords 88

- 1 Introduction 89
- 2 Theoretical Background 91
  - 2.1 *Causal Configurations in Force Theory* 91
  - 2.2 *Types of Influences* 93
- 3 Characterising Authority as a Constraint on Choice 95
  - 3.1 *Agency as Choice* 95
  - 3.2 *Constraining Agency in Complex Causatives* 97
- 4 When Syntax Matters: Structural Constraints on Authority Relations 99
  - 4.1 *Authority and Preverbal Causee* 100
  - 4.2 *Causation by Omission: Postverbal Causee* 101
  - 4.3 *Additional Evidence for the Analysis* 102
- 5 Conclusions 108

Acknowledgements 108

Index 113

Preface

This selection of papers originated as presentations at the first interdisciplinary workshop on Agency and Intentions in Language held at the Georg-August University of Goettingen in January 2021. The goal of this workshop was to bring together scholars in linguistics, philosophy, and psychology interested in questions related to agency and intentions, broadly construed. The workshop met with considerable interest from the research community and has led to a series of annual workshops.

In this selection of papers, we present some of the linguistic contributions from the workshop. On the linguistic side, the topics that were discussed at the workshop include the following: ways in which natural languages manifest different degrees of agency, the distinction between intentional and non-intentional actions (morphological marking, syntactic structures, semantic denotations of verbs and adverbials, pragmatic and contextual differences), connections between agency, intentions, and event structure and relations between agency, intentions, and causality.

The collection consists of four papers each of which focuses on a different phenomenon in a different language and also assumes a different methodology or framework. What all these contributions have in common and share with the spirit of the workshop is that they aspire to describe and then capture their respective phenomena making use of notions that are not part of the traditional conceptual palette.

The first paper 'Agency in the English Way-Construction's Constraints' by Caterina Cacioli uses a corpus data analysis to provide a more accurate description of collocations involving *way* in English, such as *dance one's way through*. The surprising finding reported in the paper is that *way*-constructions are possible with inanimate subjects contrary to what has been previously believed. This finding prompts the author to broaden the notion of agency.

The paper 'On Some Epistemic Access Effects' by Francesco Costantini focusses on what is traditionally called 'subjunctive obviation' phenomena using Italian data. Incorporating recent observations that subjunctive obviation is attested beyond subjunctive clauses, the author argues that the crucial role in the obviative/non-obviative split is played by the availability of the self-knowledge interpretation.

'Two Semantic Paths to Unintentional Causation' by Ömer Demirok investigates two constructions that are used to express unintentional actions in Laz (a South-Caucasian language). It is shown that these constructions have different empirical finger-prints and thus, should be analysed differently. The two analyses investigated by the author – modal and non-modal – are independently motivated for non-intentional constructions in other languages. The data from Laz indicate that both analyses are necessary.

In 'Letting Structure Speak with Authority' by Marta Donazzan, Clementine Raffy, Bridget Copley, and Klaus von Heusinger, two French causative constructions with *laisser* 'let' are examined. It is argued that the well-documented interpretative difference between these two constructions can be derived from their structural differences. But establishing this meaning-form connection requires looking at the primitives of causal relations, which the authors of the paper define using the force-dynamic framework.

Putting together this volume would have been impossible without the help of many people. We would like to express our profound gratitude to the reviewers who contributed their precious time and expertise to critically evaluate the papers in this collection. We would also like to sincerely thank Elisa Perotti for very efficient support during the production process and Klaus von Heusinger for proposing this publishing opportunity to us.

Julie Goncharov and Hedde Zeijlstra

Notes on Contributors

Caterina Cacioli
is a PhD student in Linguistics at the University of Florence. Her research focuses on semantics and meaning-making at the syntax-semantics interface, with experimental and empirical methodologies.

Bridget Copley
is a directrice de recherche at the lab Structures Formelles du Langage of the Centre National de la Recherche Scientifique in France. Her research interests include the natural language semantics of causation, intention, agency, and future reference. Dr. Copley runs the interdisciplinary international research network OASIS (Ontology As Structured by the Interfaces with Semantics) and the online seminar COCOA (Converging On Causal Ontology Analyses).

Francesco Costantini
is an associate professor at the University of Udine. He has conducted research on the syntax and semantics of subordination, on the syntax of infinitival clauses, and on the causative construction, with main focus on Italian and Romance languages.

Ömer Demirok
is an assistant professor at the Department of Linguistics, Boğaziçi University, Istanbul. He received his PhD in Linguistics from MIT in 2019. He has done research in formal semantics and morphosyntax, focusing on Turkish and Laz, an endangered South Caucasian language.

Marta Donazzan
is associate professor at the University of Nantes and deputy director of the Linguistics Lab (LLING). She obtained her PhD at the University of Paris 7, and has since then published on a wide variety of subjects in formal semantics, including plurality and distributivity, Tense and Aspect, and causation. She is interested in developing a formal analysis of language with respect to cross-linguistic diversity, and has recently co-directed a number of international projects investigating the realization of semantic universals in less-studied languages of the Americas.

Klaus von Heusinger
is a professor in General and German Linguistics at the University of Cologne. He works and publishes in theoretical and comparative linguistics with a focus

on referential structure, differential case marking and causative constructions in Germanic, Romance, and Turkic languages.

Clémentine Raffy
is a postdoctoral researcher at the Université Côte d'Azur (UCA) in France. Her research focuses on the natural language semantics of causation, dispositions, and Romance light verbs. She is a co-organizer of the workshop CCCA (Complement Clauses Côte d'Azur) with Friederike Moltmann, Kalle Müller, and Chang Liu.

Agency in the English Way-Construction's Constraints

Caterina Cacioli
Università degli Studi di Firenze, Italy
caterina.cacioli@unifi.it

Abstract

This study investigates the English Way-construction, as defined in Construction Grammar terms, as a case study to explore agency attribution processes at the intersection of animacy and agentive properties of verbs, on the basis of the construction's constraints previously described in literature – that the construction implies self-propelled, intentional movement and that the verb slot is restricted to unergative, agentive verbs. Corpus-based research is conducted to collect evidence of non-agentive verbs and inanimate subjects used in the construction and describe how they reconcile with the construction. The results provide a more accurate description of the way construction, showing that agency attribution processes define the construction's usage beyond its single components and relate to more general cognitive processes. On the broader picture, this study shows that the conceptualization of agency attributed to inanimate entities has consequences in the way they are accounted responsibility and seen as blameworthy.

Keywords

construction grammar – Corpus-based analysis – Way-construction – agency – animacy

1 Introduction

Research has shed light on how linguistic features or linguistic choices may be affected by the presence of agentive or non-agentive participants, animate or inanimate entities. The concept of agency, in fact, is related to intentional animate beings, capable of action, and is extended to non-volitional inanimate entities both in perception and language encoding. Disciplines other that linguistics have investigated agency, showing that inanimate entities are often attributed agency based on animacy cues – most prominently, movement and context. Even though animacy is generally not overtly marked in English, it has been shown how it still influences language, such as in the dative alternation or the genitive constructions (Bos et al. 2017; Rosenbach 2008). In addition, verbs are often described in terms of agency: in the unaccusative-unergative dichotomy, unaccusative verbs are associated with non-agentivity and the missing role of agent. The English way-construction offers the environment to investigate agency attribution at the intersection of animacy and agentive properties of the verbs.

The way-construction (exemplified in sentences 1–3), as defined within the framework of Construction Grammar (henceforth CxG), describes a movement along a path, literal or metaphorical, that is self-propelled and goal-directed:

(1) It took the forestmen about an hour to **hack their way through** the abates. (COCA, fiction, 2016)
(2) And she's not just listening to one song, she's **dancing her way through** the whole album. (COCA, ESPN, 2017)
(3) Philip Murnion [...] **whistles his way to** my office, put his arm around me and whoever else is present and tell a funny story that elicits a hearty laugh. (COCA, The Dead Live, 2009)

Previous literature has been concerned with individuating restrictions for the verb slot fillers: in syntactic accounts (Levin and Rapport 1990), the construction has been dissociated from unaccusative verbs (which notably lack self-initiation and agency) and restricted to unergative verbs, while CxG accounts (Goldberg 1995; Perek 2018) have shown that there are exceptions to the unergative verbs constraint, and that the verb class is currently extending to new verbs. However, there seems to be some gaps in the understanding of how the constraints on agentive and non-agentive verbs relate to the entities (animate and inanimate) that can participate in the construction. The entailment of self-propelled movement and the constraint for unergative verbs despite the construction being used with inanimate (unintentional and un-volitional) semantic subjects, leads to investigate two main questions: how agency is transferred to inanimate entities within the construction and to what extent unaccusative verbs are used in an agentive environment.

Within this brief description of the way-construction, there emerge that agency has a crucial role in determining the entities that fill the subject position and lemmas that fill the verb slot. However, this issue has not been explored so far: as a matter of fact, little has been said on the non-agentive verbs that are used in the construction and the variety of inanimate subject referents. In this view, the aim of this paper is to contribute to the literature on the way-construction by bringing evidence of the role that agency has in assessing the construction's potential and, in a broader view, looking at more general processes of agency attribution in language.

The remainder of this paper is structured as follows. Section 2 reports previous literature on the way-construction. Section 3 discusses the concepts of agency and animacy as they are viewed in linguistics, with particular reference to thematic roles, and as they are investigated in other disciplines. Section 3 presents and discusses the result of a corpus research. Finally, section 4 concludes and presents further opportunities for research.

2   The Way-Construction

The English way-construction has attracted the attention in CxG research for at least thirty years and has notably provided crucial evidence for the constructionist nature of language. Research on the way-construction explored its synchrony (Jackendoff 1990; Goldberg 1995), diachronic development (Israel 1996; Traugott and Trousdale 2013; Fanego 2018), as well as its relatable constructions in other Germanic languages (Mortermans and Smirnova 2020) and its distribution in World Englishes (Brunner and Hoffman 2020), but the greatest attention has been paid to exploring the verbs used in the construction, aiming at discerning those that produce acceptable from unacceptable sentences (productivity and distributional semantics, Perek 2018).

The way-construction is defined as a partially filled, non-predictable construction.[1] It is distinguished by a specific configuration of its components, described in (a) and represented with a formal schema in (b), where the oblique (OBL) codes a directional prepositional phrase:

a. Verb + Possessive Adjective + WAY + Directional Prepositional Phrase
b. [SUBJ$_i$[V [POSS$_i$ way] OBL]]. (Christy 2011; Goldberg 1995)

---

[1] In Construction Grammar, constructions range from partially filled idioms and multi-word expressions to fully abstract phrasal constructions (Perek 2018). Examples of the former would be "pull X's leg" ("pulling her leg"), "the X-er, the Y-er" ("the more the merrier") while an example of the latter would be the ditransitive construction, which is formed as NP + V + NP + NP and realised as in "he gave her a book" (Perek 2018). As a multi-word expression, the way-construction is partially filled in the sense that the form-meaning pairing has some filled components which are fix (the syntax, the noun *way*) and slots to be filled (an open class for the verb's slot, and a closed class for the possessive adjective's slot).

The construction is easily recognisable thanks to its distinctive marks: the presence of the noun *way* preceded by a possessive adjective co-referenced with the subject and followed by a prepositional phrase indicating the direction of the movement, be it literal or metaphorical:

(4)
    a.   They *made their way out* of the room.
    b.   *They made their way from the room.
(5)   They have to *make their way into* the international financial system.

Example (4a) denotes a concrete path creation and traversal, while (5) a metaphorical path. Example in (4b) shows that only directional prepositions are acceptable. In both the acceptable examples, the construction implies that a subject referent is moving along a path. It is worth pointing out that the movement implication is not achieved thanks to a verb of movement or other single parts of the construction implying movement. Examples shown so far do not include a verb of motion, despite describing a path traversal. However, this does not mean that verbs of movement are unacceptable: verbs as *walk* or *run* are used as they contribute to the movement implication with a manner component. The semantic-syntactic configuration of the construction is not negotiable, and the path-traversal implication is only conveyed under this specific configuration (see Goldberg 1995 and Perek 2018 for substitution tests).[2]

Concerning path traversal of the subject agent, there are at least three different senses (or threads, Goldberg 1995) for the construction, illustrated in examples (6–8).

(6)   I crawled my way home
(7)   I elbowed my way through the crowd
(8)   He whistles his way out of the office

In sentence (6) 'crawling one's way home' entails that crawling is the means through which the subject moves, in sentence (7) elbowing is the manner of movement. Instead, in sentence (8) whistling is an activity that incidentally occurs simultaneously with the motion but doesn't inform on the type of motion or motivates the motion[3] in literature. Diachronic studies on historical

---

2 Recalling the main tenets of CxG, linguistic knowledge is based on meaning-form patterns which form constructions composed of a single word or a string of words that taken together convey a certain meaning.
3 These senses are generally labelled means, manner, and incidental activity. However, the threads and labels are not agreed upon in the literature. There are inconsistencies in the labels given by Goldberg (1995), Israel (1996), Perek (2018), who nonetheless describe three

dictionary occurrences have evidenced that these three threads have emerged gradually, through processes of constructionalization, constructional changes, and analogical extensions (Israel 1996, Traugott and Trousdale 2013), but are now intertwined. Perek (2018) has shown, with historical and contemporary data, that the construction is currently under a process of class expansion, still increasing its productivity with newer verbs entering in use (Perek 2018). This points to the fact that the construction is expanding and that with new verbs entering, constrains might need redefining. Thus, diachronic studies and studies on the extension of the construction's productivity further motivate an investigation on the verbs that have been posited unacceptable in the construction and that may instead have entered in use.

Constraining the verbs that occur in the construction appears to be a discussed topic that poses challenges, as mentioned in section 1. The crucial work in this respect is Levin and Rappaport's (1990) classic "Unaccusativity: at the syntax-lexical semantics interface". The way-construction is here used as a diagnostic for unergativity (as opposed to unaccusativity), following Marantz (1992). Their aim is to disambiguate verbs into the said dichotomy when they show peculiarities: if unergative verbs like *cough* or *sneeze* generally indicate unintentional events, are nonetheless classified as unergative because they are acceptable and agentive in the way-construction (9).

(9) John coughed his way out of the room

Instead, verbs as *fall, die, rise* are ruled out as they are unequivocally unaccusative:

(10)
    a.   *The oil rose its way to the top
    b.   *The apples fell their way into the crates. (Levin & Rappaport 1990: 148)

Examples (10a–b) are marked as unacceptable by Levin and Rapport (1990). Interestingly, they mention animacy specifying that the reason for their unacceptability is the unaccusativity of the verb, rather than the non-agentivity of the (inanimate) subjects, as inanimate subjects can be used in the construction. Animacy is also brought into discussion by Levin and Rappaport (1990) when introducing *roll verbs*, described as a subclass of verbs of manner of motion which are not necessarily agentive. *Roll verbs* have an agentive and non-agentive

---

different threads, while, for example, Fanego (2018) distinguishes five threads (basic motion verbs, means, manner, sound emission, incidental activity).

interpretation when they are used with an animate entity, while they only have a non-agentive interpretation when used with inanimate subjects. In sentences (11a–b) the girl may intentionally or unintentionally roll, while the ball can only roll unintentionally:

(11)
    a.   the girl rolled down the hill
    b.   the ball rolled down the hill

According to Levin and Rapport (1990) *roll verbs* cannot be used in the way-construction when the subject is inanimate and thus mark (12a–b) below as unacceptable:

(12)
    a.   *The pebbles rolled their way into the stream
    b.   The children rolled their way across the field

Jackendoff (1990) contributes to this research topic constraining the construction to unbounded events: the verb must denote an ongoing process. Boundedness denotes events that come to an imminent end, while unbounded events are continuative and could possibly be perpetuated infinitely. This is not a strict property of the verbs, but rather depends on the way the action is occurring:

(13)
    a.   *She jumped *her way over* the ditch.
    b.   She jumped *her way to* the finishing line

(14)   He hiccupped *his way out of* the room.

Sentence (13b) entails a sequence of jumps and sentence (14) a sequence of hiccups. It follows that bounded events can be construed as processes, which can then occur in the construction. On the CxG side, in Goldberg's (1995) stresses the self-propelled motion component: the construction is felicitously realized when an agent performs a self-initiated movement, or when the movement is *construed* as such in the case of inanimate entities. This constraint is in line with Levin and Rappaport (1990) as it rules out those verbs that are generally classified as unaccusative. As mentioned above, Levin and Rappaport (1990) and Mondorf (2010) associate the way construction with unergative verbs only, despite counterexamples reported by Goldberg (15a–b).

(15)
    a. The planned purchase furthers Bull's strategy of trying to *grow its way out of* its extensive compute r-marketing problems. (wsj)
    b. The bank-debt restructuring is the centerpiece of Lomas Financial's months-long effort to *shrink its way back* to profitability after two straight years of heavy losses. (wsj) (Goldberg 1995: 213)

Goldberg (1995) accounts for the presence of inanimate entities in the construction positing that movement can be *construed* as self-propelled when inanimate entities are involved. Examples are reported in (16a–b).

(16)
    a. [...] sometimes it [the cyst] *forces its way out of* the [plumpton] at the top. (usda)
    b. The large seeds sprouts [...] and the strong seedlings can *push their way through* crusted soil. (usda)

(17)
    a. *The wood burned its way to the ground
    b. *The butter melted its way off the turkey. (Goldberg 1995: 213)

In sentences (16a–b) entities are forces that move in an apparent self-initiated way. Instead, examples such as (17a–b) seem to violate the self-initiation constraint, as they are marked in the literature as unacceptable.

The literature review above has highlighted the aspects that seems to define the way-construction – mainly, the verbs that are used in the construction, the self-propelled movement, and the boundedness of the event – as the construction's components that most affect the acceptability of the construction. The focus has been put in how these are linked to agency, considering that the prototypical configuration of the construction requires an agent acting intentionally but both non agentive verbs and inanimate entities are used. This suggests a need for further investigation in agency attribution processes and in the agentivity of verbs. The unaccusative-unergative dichotomy seems suitable to account for most of the occurrences but there might be a greater variety of verbs that needs to be accounted for, as also hinted at by studies on the construction's expansion in productivity. Moreover, the unacceptability marked on sentences (12a) and (17a–b) are based on intuition and introspection, while a larger investigation (e.g., on corpora) could yield different results. To frame these issues in a broader context, next section will be dedicated to introducing studies on animacy and agency in linguistics and other disciplines, focussing on how human beings conceptualize movement of inanimate entities.

3 Attributing Agency

Animacy and attribution of agency emerged as important factors from the literature reviewed in Section 2. The notion of *construed* as self-propelled movement (thus, not linked to intention or volition) opens the construction to a range of grammatical subjects which can be attributed agency.

Many linguistics frameworks have been concerned with categorizing verbs in terms of the semantic role they select. The semantic role of *agent* has been linked to intentionality and volition (Levin and Rappaport 1990) and opposed to the semantic role of *patient*. According to Dowty (1991) prototypical agents (in his terminology, *proto-agents*) exhibit properties such as:
(i)   volitional involvement in the event,
(ii) sentience,
(iii) causing an event or change of state in another participant,
(iv) movement,
(v)   exists independently of the event named by the verb.

A subject referent is more agent-like the more of these characteristics it exhibits. A different account is proposed by Functional Grammar, which distinguishes *agents* from *forces* (Dik 1997), the second being inanimate, non-controlling entities, but capable of instigating a movement or a change. Prototypical forces include natural agents (snow, rain, wind, etc.), but also collective nouns (such as organizations, when they represent a group of humans' actions). In Siewierska (1991) the notion of *forces* is also applied to animate beings involved in an accidental event. Recalling example (11), both the girl and the rock can be seen as *forces* in the accidental interpretation of the event, but only the girl can be an agent.

In other linguistic accounts, as in other disciplines, the concept of agency may be seen as decoupled from that of intentionality and from semantic roles. For example, humans often engage in activities that are unconscious or partly unconscious (Ahearn, 2010) but they would still be considered acting agentively. An account of this regard in philosophical terms comes from Ferretti and Caiani (2021), who argue for habitual actions as agentive and intentional. Duranti (2004), who has contributed greatly to this topic, does not include intentionality in the definition of agency. In Duranti (2004) agency involves entities that "(i) have some degree of control over their own behaviour,

(ii) whose actions in the world affect other entities' [actions] (and sometimes their own), and (iii) whose actions are the object of evaluation (e.g. in terms of their responsibility for a given outcome)" (Duranti, 2004:453).

Linguistics studies show how animacy in language is expressed and processed as a graded concept, rather than a dichotomy. Animacy can be displayed on a gradient hierarchy, and it may be discussed as articulated from general to specific – e.g. from bare aliveness to intentional entities (Parovel, Guidi & Kreß, 2018) – or according to semantic categorization (collective nouns, spatial and temporal nouns, concrete nouns, psychological nouns, and other abstract nouns – Ji & Liang, 2018). Regardless of the way the hierarchy is organized, it is argued that animacy is significantly influenced by the context and that it is not a rigid, fixed property of an entity. For example, collective nouns like institutions, schools, the government or a community can either be used in language in a metonymic relation to a human group of people (with agency and intentions) or representing a concrete building (Rosenbach 2008). The degree of animacy is usually accentuated in animate-coherent contexts, as evidenced in Parovel et al. (2018) and context increases the appropriateness of an inanimate entity in a generally animate linguistic environment (Nieuwland & Van Berkum, 2006). Inanimate entities are often encoded in linguistic environments that are typical for animate beings and they are spoken about in the same constructions, extending and attributing properties to non-living, inanimate entities. Languages show similar behaviour in those entities that are perceived as more agentive, as natural and supernatural phenomena (Nieuwboer, Van Schie, Karremans & Wigboldus, 2015), diseases, plants, or even technology (many studies have been carried out on the way people refer to computers – Subiaul, Vonk & Rutherford, 2011): crucially, all entities that engage in movements or actions that are not attributable to the volition of another living agent.

Views of animacy and agentivity are well captured by Van Valin and Wilkins (1996: 316): "two entities may be of the same animacy type but may be differentiated in their ability to trigger agency attribution when occurring in an actional context". Van Valin and Wilkins example is that of a rock and a tornado: they are both equally inanimate in terms of volition, but a tornado, being a force, is most likely to be treated as an agent – it has its own energy source and when it is seen in action the motion appears as self-propelled. According to this account, the three factors involved in determining whether an argument will be interpreted as an agent are the lexical-semantic properties of the verb, the lexical content of the NP argument (that is, the type of subject referent) and the grammatical construction in which they co-occur. This view accounts for an arrangement on an animacy scale from low to high of the entities that users of languages usually refer to.

Inanimate subjects are conceptualized as agentive in language in the contexts of conceptual mappings like those of metonymy, metaphors, or personifications. Objects are often introduced in a story as humanized and are attributed human characteristics, thus being acceptable in constructions that usually are preferred with animate entities. Rosenbach (2008) has shed light on a preference in English for using s-genitive with animate beings and of-genitive with inanimates, providing some evidence for animacy effects on word order as mediated by syntactic prominence and for construction-specific effects. Despite this general preference in English, when the object is found in personification or metaphorical context, the object is used with s-genitives. This phenomenon bears important implications: when an inanimate object is talked about in agentive terms and animate features are attributed, as a result, it comes to be conceptualized as intentional and/or blameworthy (a view supported by Davidson 1971).

3.1 An Effect for Movement

Inputs from other disciplines help in shedding light on how generally human beings attribute and perceive agency and intentionality. The typical characteristic of animate entities that is most often associated with agentivity is the ability to volitionally initiating a movement. Movement is often present in the discussion on agentivity in multi-disciplinary perspectives as a cue to animacy. In the case of motion events, and motion constructions in particular, inanimate entities are extended in place of auto-causative events. A first significant and seminal work is that of Heider and Simmel (1944), in which it is proven that agency is attributed to simple geometrical shapes, followed by evidence for two- and three-dimensional objects (Buren & Scholl 2017). The perception of animacy in objects in motions has been related to the apparent self-propelled motion in the absence of an external cause to attribute the motion to – when there is not an overt source of energy that is easily identifiable as the causer of the motion (Premack, 1990; Gelman, Durgin, & Kaufman, 1995; Tremoulet & Feldman, 2000). Moreover, as proven by Barret and Johnson (2003), people are more inclined to attribute animacy when the action is perceived as outside their own agency (for example, when not able to control a computer or a machine: e.g. "the computer is) and when the object appears to move in a self-propelled, goal-directed way. There is a robust and coherent body of literature showing that agentivity is attributed when the event is visually goal-directed (Tremoulet & Feldman, 2006; Gao, McCarthy, & Scholl, 2010; Lee, Gao, & McCarthy, 2014), also suggesting that it might be a universal component of human cognition (Barrett, Todd, Miller & Blythe, 2005). In fact, agency attribution strategies cued by movement emerge early in children, as shown by Barret and Johnson (2003) and more recently by Hofrichter, Mueller and Rutherford (2021) who compared animacy attribution between adults and children.

Strong evidence for attribution of agency and the cognitive perception of movements comes from neuroscience. Using functional magnetic resonance imaging (fMRI), it is found that vision of animate and inanimate entities activates two different neural responses (Santos, Kuzmanovic, David, et al. 2010; Naselaris, Stansbury & Gallant 2012) but that when a two-dimensional object appears to engage in a chasing activity (thus, moving), the neural response is the same as for animate entities (activity in the posterior superior temporal sulcus – Lee, Gao & McCarthy 2014). These results suggest that specific areas of the brain mediate perception of agency independently of the actual animacy of the entity due to an effect of animacy cues such as movement.

The findings presented above result from experimental paradigms in which perception of animacy is assessed employing judgements or rating tasks, relying on visual experiments, or investigating neural responses. Taking section 3 inputs altogether, there is evidence from linguistics, psychology, neurosciences, and behavioural studies that movement and context are cues to the attribution of agentivity to inanimate entities. Thus, what happens in language with the attribution of agency to inanimate entities and consequent use in constructions that requires agentivity is to be related to more general cognitive processes. Conceptual mappings as metonymy, metaphor or personification enable the association of inanimate entities with agent-like properties in language and linguistic choices reflect the conceptualization of the speakers of inanimates as more or less agentive. This last point is important in cross-disciplinary studies, as attributing agency to an inanimate entity through language encoding may lead speakers to conceptualize an entity (object, natural force, institution, organization, etc.) as responsible for some events or blameworthy, with positive or negative implications (such as lifting responsibility from other human beings or blaming institutions rather than individuals).

For the reasons discussed in this and the previous section, next section is concerned with investigating agency in the English way-construction, particularly suitable for the topic since it has a strong motion entailment and involves a self-propelled movement, a cue to animacy.

4 Corpus Research and Analysis

As anticipated in section 1, this study uses a corpus-based approach, building on previous studies, analyzing occurrences in order to explore the range of verbs and inanimate entities that are used in the way-construction in naturally-occurring environments. This means using data that does not come from introspection, intuition or elicitation. On the contrary, the interest is to collect already produced utterances to investigate actual usage.

4.1 *Method*

Two different corpora have been used to gather a large quantity of data and obtain a comprehensive view of the verbs in the way-construction, and, in particular, the non-agentive verbs and the inanimate entities involved. The first corpus, COCA, is used for its representativity and to have a general overview of the construction in a contemporary corpus: it allowed to gather a large quantity of data to capture variation in prototypical, conventional uses and the creative or novel ones. Considering the limited size of COCA and the marginality of the construction in the corpus, a second corpus (larger, more recent) has been consulted to search for specific non agentive uses of the construction – the iWeb.

Both corpora were accessed through the *English-corpora.org* interface. The COCA, Corpus of Contemporary American English (COCA – Davies, 2008–), is a 560 million words corpus gathering American English texts and transcriptions of spoken American English divided per 5 genres (fiction, popular magazines, newspapers, and academic texts) with the same amount of text per genre and per year. Thus, it is a balanced corpora in terms of genre of the text and data per year, covering the period from 1990 to 2017. As the COCA is a relatively small-sized corpus to capture smaller-scale phenomena of language use, the iWeb (Davies, 2018) was also used to gather occurrences of the way-construction. The iWeb corpus contains 14 billion words (25 times the size of COCA), gathered from 22 million web pages and English varieties from 6 countries. With the iWeb, it is possible to capture more extensions and novel uses.

Given the formulaic nature of the construction, the search was conducted using pos-tags to delimit the outcome. The research string used was:

_v* _app* way _i*

The string can be made explicit as: verb as lemma, possessive adjective, way, preposition. This research string was considerably accurate, but occurrences

returned did not meet all criteria to be qualified as an occurrence of the way-construction. The criteria, based on Perek (2018) and Goldberg (1995) were the following:
(i) way is followed by a PP which describes a path of motion (literal or metaphorical);
(ii) the clause entails motion of the subject referent, the means through which motion is enabled, the manner of motion or an incidental action performed by the subject referent during motion.

The search was thus refined manually in order to eliminate duplicate sentences and select only directional prepositions. Cases of polysemy (e.g., "road trip your way across the whole continent", "day trip your day around") and occurrences in which there was no sense of movement implied were excluded (e.g., 'show your way to').

4.2 Results

The search returned approximately 23,000 occurrences and the final, refined sample included 21,000 occurrences and 1114 type verbs. To give an overview on the way-construction, it is worth mentioning briefly what emerges from the COCA in terms of genres, verb frequencies and preposition types. The construction is mainly found in fictional texts (Figure 1), accounting for almost half of the occurrences, while academic prose is the least frequent genre.

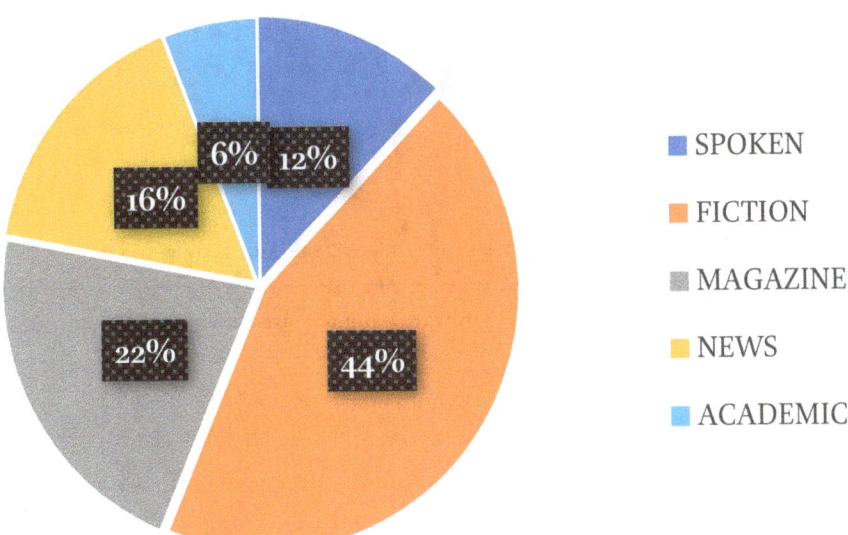

FIGURE 1   Pie chart showing the distribution of occurrences per text genre in the COCA (Davies, 2008–)

Looking at the five most frequent verbs, there emerge that they all denote a movement along a path that is being created (*work, make, find*) by the agent, occasionally with an obstacle (*push, fight*). This, in accordance with findings from Goldberg (1995) and Perek (2018), is the most conventional use of the construction and shows the construction is strongly associated with an intentional agent.

The most frequent prepositions are *through* (24.80%) *to* (23.49%) and *into* (14.87%), which encode the direction of the action carried out by the agent. Prepositions always encode the direction, and although they vary, there also emerge some verb-preposition preference (Table 1) for reasons of semantic coherence (Stefanowitsch and Gries 2005) or influenced by other collocations. For example, *talk and* buy mostly occurs with *into* (respectively, 42% and 43%) and *out* (respectively, 42% and 40%), *pay* and *cut* with *through* (respectively, 56% and 43%), *think through* (37%) and *grow out* (89%).

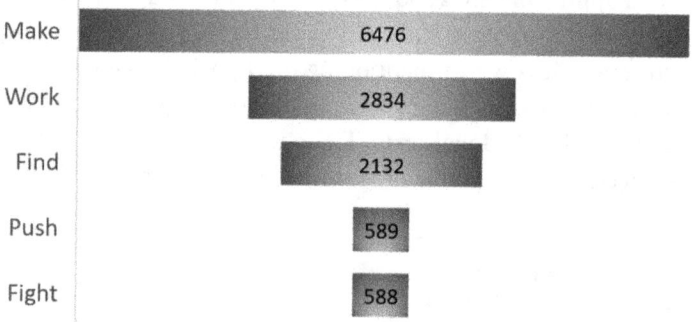

FIGURE 2   Five most frequent verbs in the way-construction attested in COCA (Davies 2008–)

TABLE 1   Raw frequencies of verbs with prepositions in the COCA (Davies, 2008)

	up	down	around	across	toward	along	past	into	to	through	out
Talk	2		6		1		12	123	4	18	122
Buy	2							77	23	2	72
Pay		1						9	32	69	11
Cut	2	2			1			4	17	33	17
Think			8					8	8	24	17
Grow								3	2		42

TABLE 2   COCA raw frequencies for verbs occurring in the way-construction

COCA	Raw frequency	COCA	Raw frequency
Stumble	58	Grow	72
Roll	12	Shrink	2
Tumble	4	Melt	10
Trip	3	Burn	21

Moving to what concerns agency, a set of unaccusative and non-agentive verbs as they occur in the COCA are reported in Table 2. As predicted in the literature, strongly unaccusative verbs such as *arrive, show, fall, die, rise* are ot attested.

The search on the iWeb, given the difference in size compared to the COCA, returned more occurrences to investigate this set of verbs (Table 3). Being the construction mostly used in fiction and magazines, as Figure 1 shows, a web corpus that gathers blogs and fictional web pages is a suitable source. Verbs chosen to be investigated more closely are unaccusative verbs (*grow, shrink, melt, burn, die, fall*), verbs that are generally non-agentive but have a manner component (*stumble, trip*) and the verbs discussed in literature which have an intentional and unintentional reading (*roll, tumble*) (Levin and Rappaport 1990). Occurrences from the iWeb were manually annotated distinguishing animate and inanimate entities on gradient scale – human subjects, animals, groups, organizations and institutions, natural phenomena, other objects – following previous works on annotation (Bos et al., 2017 for separating human subjects from organizations and institutions). Further annotation included distinguishing between concrete and abstract occurrences. Table 3 shows the total number of occurrences per verb, the frequency of inanimate entities, concrete uses, and concrete inanimate uses. The last column lists the most frequent types of inanimate entities.

Results from the annotation revealed differences in the abstract-concrete and animate-inanimate distribution between verbs. *Stumble* is the most frequent among this set of verbs, occurring mostly with animate subjects and in abstract senses. Within the inanimate ones, none is used in a concrete construct. *Stumble* is listed among agentive verbs of manner of motion by Levin and Rappaport (1995) but considered unaccusative (Perlmutter, 1975), unaccusative with a manner component (Narasimhan et al., 1996) and non-agentive (Pross, 2020) in other accounts. It has an evident manner component, and it can be construed as an iterative motion, making it a valid candidate to

TABLE 3 Raw frequencies in the iWeb Corpus (Davies, 2018) with raw number and percentage of inanimate entities, concrete uses and inanimate-concrete uses (percentage based on concrete uses' raw frequency). On the last column: categories of inanimate subjects attested with the corresponding verb. Organizations include institutions, government, teams, bands, buildings (ex: school, the white house, 'the lakers'); media products include songs, movies, episode of tv series, tv shows; abstract concepts include thoughts, ideas, feelings and sensations.

Verb	Raw frequency	Inanimate entities	Concrete uses	Concrete inanimate	Type inanimate entity
Stumble	553	16 (2.9%)	75 (13.6%)	0	Organizations, media product, technology
Roll	195	37 (19%)	93 (47.7%)	18 (19.3%)	Wheeled machines, round objects, teams, media product
Tumble	40	2 (5%)	28 (70%)	1 (3.6%)	Glaciers, means of transportation
Trip	13	2 (15.4%)	3 (23%)	0	Media product, power.
Grow	270	117 (43.3%)	8 (3%)	6 (75%)	Government, country, market, economy, business, plants.
Shrink	26	6 (23%)	0	0	Company, technology, media product, country.
Melt	79	60 (78%)	69 (87.3%)	59 (85.5%)	Nuclear reactor, lava, substances and chemical agents, ice.
Burn	228	109 (48.2%)	103 (45.2%)	52 (50.5%)	Tools, chemical products, fire, flame, nuclear reactor, abstract concepts.
Fall	9	1 (11.1%)	8 (88.9%)	0	Media product
Rise	6	0	0	0	
Die	6	1 (16.7%)	0	0	Media product

participate in the construction. The occurrences show that although denoting a motion that is usually not performed volitionally or not necessarily internally caused, it does not conflict with the self-propelled motion constraint. In fact, it implies a manner of movement that is *un*intentional during an intentional path traversal:

(18)
    a. As I *stumble my way through* Dublin city center, I finally catch a sight of her.
    b. "[…] I *stumbled my way through* the streets of Naples". (iWeb, happyblackwoman.com)

c. As long as they're not *stumbling their way into* my car, I don't mind giving them a ride. (iWeb, therideshareguy.com)
d. And at the end of the night, you help everyone *stumble their way to* the car, and you drive them home. (iWeb, scholarshippoints.com)

In sentences (18a–d) the verb denotes a clumsy or unsteady movement that happens to occur during an intended path traversal. In sentence (19a) and (19b), the stumbling is metaphorical and refers to the subject referent not knowing the place they're visiting and thus moving unconfidently around. Sentences (18c) and (18d) have a more concrete sense. In a similar vein, although with lower raw frequency, *trip* is mostly used with animate subjects. It is hypothesized here that due to its polysemy it is less apt to enter the construction systematically.

Inanimate entities are more consistently found with *melt*, in 78% of the occurrences, while animates in *grow* and *burn* account for almost half of the occurrences. *Melt* has mainly a concrete use, but this is not typical of any other verb. In fact, abstract uses seem to be preferred, confirming the fictional, evocative character of the construction. *Melt* is attested in contexts of a subject referent moving by means of melting, or intrinsically able to cause melting (mainly, tools and machines), rather than subjects able to undergo a melting process (20–22). This aspect confirms that the construction is constructed on agentive premises, that are attributed to inanimate entities.

(19) A hot water drill will *melt its way through* the frozen ice. (iWeb, geographypods.com)
(20) Magma is *melting its way through* the icecap producing a circular ice free area. (iWeb, volcanolive.com)
(21) From making the purest meth in New Mexico to using Etch-a-Sketch powder to *melt his way into* a warehouse, Walt knows how to make his subject work. (iWeb, www.cnet.com)[4]

In (20–22) the subject referents are two inanimate entities and one animate entity: a tool ('hot water drill, sentence 20), a semi-liquid substance ('magma', sentence 21) and a human being ('Walt', 22). Interestingly, only the subject in (22) has the actual properties of the semantic role of agent and only (21) has the physical properties needed to create a path by a melting process. They display different degrees of animacy but are all conceptualized as creating a path.

---

4 This occurrence might need contextual clarification: here, the subject of the way construction is *Walt*: melting refers to the character using a substance to melt a door lock and make his way into a building.

The unaccusative *grow*, reported by Goldberg (1995) to be an exception to Levin and Rappaport's (1990) unergative constraint, describes physical and abstract growth. In terms of types of inanimate participants, *grow* has the highest coherence: the entities attested can be all grouped in few categories. With *grow*, 60% of the occurrences refer to a nation 'making their way out of debt', and another 29% are other types of entities (government, the economy, the market, university) in the same context. Physical growth is marginal and occurs with humans (25) or plants (26). As pointed out above, the most frequent use is that of 'growing one's way out of debt' (22–23), for abstract entities as 'the economy' or 'the market' or for companies, countries, cities, organizations. Abstract growth concerning animate entities is also attested, as in example (24).

(22) Don't expect the US economy to *grow its way out* of debt. (iWeb, investingdaily.com)
(23) Spending growth was controlled, and the economy was allowed to *grow its way out* of debt. (iWeb, mauldineconomics.com)
(24) We have been left with so much debt we can't just *grow our way out* of it – we should consider a radical option. (iWeb, econintersect.com)
(25) I *grew my way through* V8 Supercars so I was the director of sport and operations. (iWeb, www.qt.com.au)
(26) The lily will *grow its way across* the pot. (iWeb, gardenpondforum.com)

These results show that *grow* has established uses, with animate and inanimate entities. *Grow* has a strong semantic consistency in the domain of economic growth and it is almost exclusively used with the directional path expressed by *out of* ('grow our way out of debt'), suggesting that it extended to constitute a fixed subschema of the construction or a strong collocational preference.

On the contrary, *burn* is attested with a wider variety of entities and semantic contexts: tools used to 'burn one's way' account for 10% of the occurrences and are the most frequent coherent category, followed by abstract uses (ideas, thoughts, feelings, words) as in examples (27–29), with occurrences involving fire and flames, rocket, lava, acid, fuel, cigarettes, concrete inflammable objects (pieces of paper, documents).

(27) It sounds like you have an idea *burning its way through* your head. (iWeb, www.metronews.ca)
(28) [...] but one thought *burns its way through* his mind and into his mouth. (iWeb, penguinmagic.com)
(29) Every word seemed to *burn its way into* my heart. (iWeb, www.theregister.co.uk)

Roll and *tumble* are part of Levin and Rapport's *roll verbs*, that are described as unacceptable in the way-construction when combined with an inanimate subject. Corpus data show occurrences of inanimate subjects with these verbs, as reported in (30–31), in both concrete and abstract senses:

(30)
- a. A wave of mud *rolled its way inside* her boots. (iWeb, many books4u.net)
- b. RocketSkates by Acton are *rolling their way into* the world of wearable technology. (iWeb, urbanwearables.technology)
- c. The Elvis Express will *roll its way from* Sydney to Parkes. (iWeb, graceland.com)
- d. and looks down to see a small jar *rolling its way towards* him. (iWeb, simplyscripts.com)

(31) So why are there glaciers *tumbling their way through* the jungle in the first place? (iWeb, gadling.com)

Inanimate entities attested with *roll* are wheeled machines or objects in the measure of 30%. Among the metonymic uses there is also consistent evidence of the verb used to denote the movement of a part of the subject referent, as in (32a) where rolling refers to the wheels, also extended to metaphorical rolling (32b):

(32)
- a. [...] as the cart *rolled its way to* the palace. (iWeb, janicehardy.com)
- b. the '66 T-bird convertible *has rolled its way to* fame in several other films. (iWeb, history.com)

Fall, die, rise are strongly unaccusative verbs and have been excluded from descriptive accounts of the way-construction unanimously. The iWeb shows occurrences of these verbs, construed as processes:

(33) Stumble, fumbled, and *fell her way up* the hill towards her sister. (iWeb, endlessforest.org)

(34)
- a. [...] was to stay out of the way as my children *fell their way to* standing. (iWeb, corewalking.com)
- b. [...] every time they tripped over a step and *fell their way up to* the 18-foot-high entrance. (iWeb, irishecho.com)

(35) He spent his entire career at the bank, eventually *rising his way to* the top as president. (iWeb, streakingthelawn.com)

(36) I don't mind *dying my way through* a dungeon and I enjoy a FAIR challenge. (iWeb, ddo.com)

They are limited to specific contexts – for example, *die* appears in fictional prose or in the narration of actions performed by characters of video games or tv shows. In the above examples, the unaccusative verbs are construed as reiterative, denoting a continuative process – as the abstract sense of sentence (35), climbing to higher positions during a career path – or on a more concrete base, learning to stand by means of falling many times (34a).

4.3 Discussion

Examining the construction's most frequent types of occurrences from a balanced corpus of English and taking into consideration the most frequent verbs, it emerges the strong component of intentional creation of a path or path traversal:

(37)
   a. Travis got up and *made his way to* the refrigerator. (COCA, Bk:WorldMadeStraight, 2017)
   b. She thought she'd *work her way to* the front door. (COCA, Bk:TrueBetrayals, 1995)
   c. I *push my way to* the front of the crowd and see Jeff waving his arms. (COCA, Ploughshares, 1999)
   d. He was an electrical engineer and *worked his way through* college going to night school and fixing radios. (COCA, NPR Talk Nations, 2009)

Thus, as noted in previous literature, unergative verbs are the most frequent participants in this construction, implying the agentivity of a subject engaged in a self-propelled action, coupled with intentionality. The general trend is thus that in its most frequent occurrences and prototypical configuration, the subject of the way-construction is involved in the creation of a path expressed with an unergative verb and in intentional contexts. However, corpus data show that the syntactic-semantic constraint excluding unaccusative verbs or the constraint to self-propelled, volitional motion are less restrictive than described in the literature. Verbs such as *grow* and *shrink* (as firstly pointed out by Goldberg 1995) are attested in corpora along with *fall*, *die* and *rise*, but also *melt* and *burn*. A group of these verbs is attested more consistently than others (*stumble, grow, roll, burn*), and the qualitative investigation shows that these are more established in the construction – being used consistently in a specific domain or with a specific preposition (*grow out*). Having found evidence for a great variety of verbs that are prototypically non-agentive shows that these verbs have an agentive interpretation if used in an appropriate context, as that of the way-construction: it has been shown that the construction itself (as defined in CxG) involves movement and intentionality beyond the single components (that is, the single words composing the construction). As a result, it emerges that agentivity is not inherently possessed by verbs and is mediated through constructions: in the case of *stumble*, only used with animate entities, usually denoting an unintentional movement, the subjects retain their agency (volitional and intentional) in the initiation of the movement, only less so in the manner of movement. On a similar vein, occurrences with non-agentive verbs such as *grow* and *shrink*, take the construction further from the prototype and show how non agentive verbs can also be paired with inanimate entities and still produce acceptable sentences. In the specific cases of these two verbs, they are not sparse occurrences but fixed subschemas of the construction. Inanimate entities (from plants to diseases to the economy) are thus conceptualized as agentive, initiating the process of growing, shrinking and also rolling. *Roll* verbs were especially interesting as far as agency is concerned: it is found counterevidence to Levin and Rapport (1995) exclusion of inanimate entities to cooccur with *roll* verbs in the way-construction. Examples (32a–b) involve inanimate entities. Verbs such as fall, die and rise, in the way they occur in the corpus, take the construction even further from the prototypical configuration and display a high degree of abstraction. Moreover, the set of verbs closely investigated here differed in the way they are paired with inanimate entities: verbs like *stumble*, *trip* and *fall* are semantically close to human activities and only personified inanimate entities may be suitable, while *melt* and *burn* better fit a context in which the subject referent is inanimate, showing that agency attribution and agentivity works together with the semantic context.

The focus on agency in the way-construction has driven a cross-disciplinary review of agency attribution processes showing a general cognitive tendency for agency attribution based on cues such as movement and context. This has motivated interpreting the construction entailment of self-propelled motion for inanimate entities as related to more general cognitive processes. For inanimate entities to be attributed agency the motion needs to be cognitively processed – and processable – as self-propelled, on the basis of a lack of other overt initiators of the motion and in accordance with the context. This reconciles with Van Valin and Wilkins (2001) account (and other accounts as Parovel et al. 2018 and Rosenbach, 2008) according to which inanimate entities are differentiated in the agency attributions they trigger depending on the actional context: the way-construction provides the context for triggering animacy attribution of entities that appear to perpetuate an auto-causative movement or abstract ones conceptualized as traversing a path. Concrete objects, which stand lower on the animacy scale, that in the way-construction triggers animacy are often round objects or wheeled objects, which are structurally able to perpetuate a movement and prompting perceived self-propelled movement. As this shows how context influences animacy attribution (all concrete objects are equally inanimate but there are contextual reasons for some of them to be more likely to be found in the construction) it should also be highlighted that other inanimate entities that do not meet the round objects criteria are attested, as listed in table 3. In particular, inanimate entities more easily constructed as self-propelled, and thus more frequently attested, are organizations and institutions ('the school', 'the government', 'the UK'), but also intellectual products (a book, a movie, a tv show) or physical products used in abstract senses to describe a path whose creator is concealed. As far as institutions are concerned, they are higher in the animacy hierarchy, being composed on people and assolve the function, discussed in section 3, of passing responsibility and decision-making. Concerning other products, example (38) shows how a food product is conceptualized as the motion along a path created by the product itself, in lack of an over causer of the action (maybe consumers' choices or marketing strategies).

(38) The doughnut quickly *worked its way into* American culture. (COCA, SanFranChron, 2004)

Finally, these results are taken to show that linguistic constraints based on verb classes or dichotomous verb types seems to be unsuitable to account for the variation and creativity of language. Agency is not necessarily embedded in the verb but is more dynamic. The dynamicity is achieved through cognitive processes of agency attribution and reflected in language use.

5   Conclusions

This paper discussed the way-construction's constraints on verbs and inanimate entities focusing on agency as the feature that could help describing the construction's uses and extensions. Using evidence from corpora, it has been shown that the constraints that characterize the construction are not fully captured by the unergative-unaccusative dichotomy, while focussing on agentivity allowed to better account for the variety of verbs and subject entities, and the interplay between them. The construction lends itself to be used with inanimate entities which are conceptualized as agentive in accordance to more general cognitive-perceptual attribution strategies (context, apparent self-propelled movement, lack of an overt causer of the movement). This study contributes to the research on the way-construction and to CxG research, bringing further evidence of the form-meaning nature of constructions as not defined by their single components but only analysable as a unit: it has proven unsuitable to constraint the single parts of the way-construction, such as verbs, in terms of their general lexical meaning or dichotomous distinctions. More to the point, this study contributes to the understanding of agency attribution, as a phenomenon observable in language, showing that is motivated by more general cognitive processes. Taking these two contributions together, we conclude that agency is a necessary concept to take into consideration in investigating the way-construction and that agency in language should be investigated going beyond verbs or single components of a construction. It is better understood if framed into context and related cognitive processes: quoting Enfield (2015), "only when we frame language in terms of agency we will properly understand the ways in which it is used to create social reality". We can relate to this for the broader conclusions of our work: that the conceptualization of agency attributed to inanimate entities has major consequences about the way we interpret reality. Inanimate entities are seen as responsible and blameworthy, which results in lifting responsibility from an actual (covert or overt) entity, such as institutions, organizations or material objects (e.g., "the funds were suspected of having found their way into off-shore bank accounts") or other processes in culture and society (e.g., "the bill is working its way through the Senate"). Further research on this topic should then be oriented at gathering experimental data on people's perception of agency in linguistic constructions and judgements on responsibility and blame.

References

Ahearn, Laura M. (2010). Agency and language. *Handbook of Pragmatics*, 14, 1–25.

Barrett, H. Clark, Todd, Peter M., Miller, Geoffrey F., & Blythe, Philip W. (2005). Accurate judgments of intention from motion cues alone: A cross-cultural study. *Evolution and Human Behavior*, 26(4), 313–331.

Brunner, Thomas, & Hoffmann, Thomas. (2020). The way-construction in World Englishes*. *English World-Wide. A Journal of Varieties of English*, 41(1), 1–32.

Bos, Johan, Basile, Valerio, Evang, Kilian, Venhuizen, Noortje J., & Bjerva, Johannes. (2017). The Groningen Meaning Bank. In N. Ide & J. Pustejovsky (Eds.), Handbook of Linguistic Annotation. Dordrecht: Springer.

Christie, Elizabeth. (2011). Investigating the Differences Between the English Way-Construction and the Fake Reflexive Resultative Construction. *Proceedings of the 2011 Annual Conference of the Canadian Linguistic Association*, 1997, 1–14.

Davidson, Donald. (1971). Agency. In A. R. N. Marras, R. Bronaugh, & R. W. Binkeley (Eds.), *Agent, Action, and Reason*. University of Toronto Press.

Davies, Mark. (2008–) The Corpus of Contemporary American English (COCA). Available online at http://corpus.byu.edu/coca/. Accessed 18/05/2020.

Davies, Mark. (2018) The iWeb Corpus. Available online at https://www.english-corpora.org/iWeb/. Accessed 18/05/2020.

Dik, Simon C. (1997). *The Theory of Functional Grammar: The structure of the clause* (K. Hengeveld (Ed.); second, revised). Berlin: Mouton de Gruyter.

Dowty, David. (1991). Thematic Proto-Roles and Argument Selection. *Language*, 67(3), 547–619.

Duranti, Alessandro. (2004). Agency in Language. In A. Duranti (Ed.), *A Companion to Linguistic Anthropology*. Malden: Blackwell Publishing.

Enfield, N. J. (2015). Linguistic Relativity from Reference to Agency. *Annual Review of Anthropology*, 44(1), 207–224.

Fanego, Teresa. (2018). A construction of independent means: The history of the Way construction revisited. *English Language and Linguistics*, 23(3), 671–699.

Ferretti, Gabriele, & Zipoli Caiani, Silvano. (2021). Habitual Actions, Propositional Knowledge, Motor Representations and Intentionality. *Topoi*, 1, 3, 623–635.

Gao, Tao, McCarthy, Gregory, & Scholl, Brian J. (2010). The wolfpack effect: Perception of animacy irresistibly influences interactive behavior. *Psychological Science*, 21(12), 1845–1853.

Gelman, Rochel, Durgin, Frank, & Kaufman, Lisa. (1995). Distinguishing between animates and inanimates: not by motion alone. In D. Sperberg, D. Premack, & A. J. Premack (Eds.), *Causal Cognition – A multidisciplinary debate* (pp. 150–184). New York: Clarendon Press.

Goldberg, Adele E. (1995). *A Construction Grammar Approach to Argument Structure*. Chicago: The University of Chicago Press.

Goldberg, Adele E. (2006). *Constructions at Work. The Nature of Generalization in Language*. Oxford: Oxford University Press.

Heider, Fritz, & Simmel, Marianne. (1944). An Experimental Study of Apparent Behavior. *The American Journal of Psychology*, 57(2), 259.

Hofrichter, Ruth, Mueller, Megan E., & Rutherford, M. D. (2021). Children's Perception of Animacy: Social Attributions to Moving Figures. *Perception*, 50(5), 387–398.

Israel, Michael. (1996). The way constructions grow. *Conceptual Structure, Discourse and Language*, 217, 217–230.

Jackendoff, Ray S. (1990). *Semantic Structures*. Cambridge (MA): The MIT press.

Ji, Jie, & Liang, Maocheng. (2018). An animacy hierarchy within inanimate nouns: English corpus evidence from a prototypical perspective. *Lingua*, 205, 71–89.

Lee, Su Mei, Gao, Tao, & McCarthy, Gregory. (2014). Attributing intentions to random motion engages the posterior superior temporal sulcus. *Social Cognitive and Affective Neuroscience*, 9(1), 81–87.

Levin, Beth, & Rappaport Hovav, Malka. (1995). *Unaccusativity: at the syntax-lexical semantics interface*. Cambridge (MA): The MIT press.

Marantz, Alec (1992). The Way-Construction and the Semantics of Direct Arguments in English: A Reply to Jackendoff. In T. Stowell & E. Wehrili (Eds.), Syntax and the Lexicon (pp. 179–188). Leiden: Brill.

Mondorf, Britta. (2010). Variation and change in English resultative constructions. *Language Variation and Change*, 22(3), 397–421.

Mortelmans, Tania, & Smirnova, Elena. (2020). Analogues of the way-construction in German and Dutch: Another Germanic sandwich? In *German and Dutch in Contrast: Synchronic, Diachronic and Psycholinguistic Perspectives* (pp. 47–76). Berlin, Boston: De Gruyter.

Narasimhan, Bhuvana, Di Tomaso, Vittorio, & Verspoor, Cornelia M. (1996). *Unaccusative or Unergative? Verbs of Manner of Motion*. Quaderni del laboratorio di Linguistica 10.

Naselaris, Thomas, Stansbury, Dustin E., & Gallant, Jack L. (2012). Cortical representation of animate and inanimate objects in complex natural scenes. *Journal of Physiology Paris*, 106(5–6), 239–249.

Nieuwboer, Wieteke, van Schie, Hein T., Karremans, Johan C., & Wigboldus, Daniel H. J. (2015). Supernatural Agency and Forgiveness. *Journal for the Cognitive Science of Religion*, 3(1), 85–100.

Nieuwland, Mante S., & Van Berkum, Jos J. A. (2006). When peanuts fall in love: N400 evidence for the power of discourse. *Journal of Cognitive Neuroscience*, 18(7), 1098–1111.

Parovel, Giulia, Guidi, Stefano, & Kreß, Karina. (2018). Different contexts change the impression of animacy. *Attention, Perception, and Psychophysics*, 80(2), 553–563.

Perlmutter, David M. (1978). Impersonal Passives and the Unaccusative Hypothesis. Proceedings of the Annual Meeting of the Berkeley Linguistics Society, 157–189.

Perek, Florent. (2018). Recent change in the productivity and schematicity of the way-construction: A distributional semantic analysis. *Corpus Linguistics and Linguistic Theory*, 14(1), 65–97.

Premack, David. (1990). The infant's theory of self-propelled objects. *Cognition*, 36(1), 1–16.

Pross, Tillman. (2020). Distributional semantics and the conceptual foundations of verb meaning: How neural word embeddings memorize the unaccusative hypothesis. In C. Pinon & L. Roussarie (Eds.), Empirical Issues in Syntax and Semantics 13.

Rosenbach, Annette. (2008). Animacy and grammatical variation – Findings from English genitive variation. *Lingua*, 118(2), 151–171.

Santos, Natacha S., Kuzmanovic, Bojana, David, Nicole, Rotarska-Jagiela, A., Eickhoff, Simon B., Shah, J. N., Fink, G. R., Bente, Gary, & Vogeley, Kai. (2010). Animated brain: A functional neuroimaging study on animacy experience. *NeuroImage*, 53(1), 291–302.

Siewierska, Anna. (1991). *Functional grammar*. London, New York: Routledge.

Stefanowitsch, Anatol., & Gries, Stefan T. (2005). Covarying collexemes. *Corpus Linguistics and Linguistic Theory*, 1(1), 1–43.

Subiaul, Francys, Vonk, Jennifer, & Rutherford, M. D. (2011). The ghosts in the computer: The role of agency and animacy attributions in "Ghost Controls." *PLoS ONE*, 6(11), e26429.

Traugott, Elizabeth, & Trousdale, Graeme (2013). Constructionalization and Constructional Changes. In *Oxford Studies in Diachronic and Historical Linguistics*. Oxford: Oxford University Press.

Traugott, Elizabeth, & Trousdale, Graeme. (2013). Constructionalization and Constructional Changes. Oxford: Oxford University Press.

Tremoulet, Patrice D., & Feldman, Jacob. (2000). Perception of animacy from the motion of a single object. *Perception*, 29(8), 943–951.

Tremoulet, Patrice D., & Feldman, Jacob. (2006). The influence of spatial context and the role of intentionality in the interpretation of animacy from motion. *Perception and Psychophysics*, 68(6), 1047–1058.

Van Buren, Benjamin, & Scholl, Brian J. (2017). Minds in motion in memory: Enhanced spatial memory driven by the perceived animacy of simple shapes. *Cognition*, 163, 87–92.

Van Valin, Robert D. (2001). *An Introduction to Syntax*. Cambridge: Cambridge University Press.

Van Valin, Robert D., & Wilkins, David. (1996). The Case for "Effector": Case Roles, Agents and Agency Revisited. In M. Shibatani & S. Thompson (Eds.), *Grammatical Constructions*. New York: Clarendon Press.

contributes to the research on the way-construction and to CxG research, bringing further evidence of the form-meaning nature of constructions as not defined by their single components but only analysable as a unit: it has proven unsuitable to constrain the single parts of the way-construction, such as verbs, in terms of their general lexical meaning or dichotomous distinctions. More to the point, this study contributes to the understanding of agency attribution, as a phenomenon observable in language, showing that is motivated by more general cognitive processes. Taking these two contributions together, we conclude that agency is a necessary concept to take into consideration in investigating the way-construction and that agency in language should be investigated going beyond verbs or single components of a construction. It is better understood if framed into context and related cognitive processes: quoting Enfield (2015), "only when we frame language in terms of agency we will properly understand the ways in which it is used to create social reality". We can relate to this for the broader conclusions of our work: that the conceptualization of agency attributed to inanimate entities has major consequences about the way we interpret reality. Inanimate entities are seen as responsible and blameworthy, which results in lifting responsibility from an actual (covert or overt) entity, such as institutions, organizations or material objects (e.g., "the funds were suspected of having found their way into off-shore bank accounts") or other processes in culture and society (e.g., "the bill is working its way through the Senate"). Further research on this topic should then be oriented at gathering experimental data on people's perception of agency in linguistic constructions and judgements on responsibility and blame.

References

Ahearn, Laura M. (2010). Agency and language. *Handbook of Pragmatics*, 14, 1–25.
Barrett, H. Clark, Todd, Peter M., Miller, Geoffrey F., & Blythe, Philip W. (2005). Accurate judgments of intention from motion cues alone: A cross-cultural study. *Evolution and Human Behavior*, 26(4), 313–331.
Brunner, Thomas, & Hoffmann, Thomas. (2020). The way-construction in World Englishes*. *English World-Wide. A Journal of Varieties of English*, 41(1), 1–32.
Bos, Johan, Basile, Valerio, Evang, Kilian, Venhuizen, Noortje J., & Bjerva, Johannes. (2017). The Groningen Meaning Bank. In N. Ide & J. Pustejovsky (Eds.), Handbook of Linguistic Annotation. Dordrecht: Springer.
Christie, Elizabeth. (2011). Investigating the Differences Between the English Way-Construction and the Fake Reflexive Resultative Construction. *Proceedings of the 2011 Annual Conference of the Canadian Linguistic Association*, 1997, 1–14.

Davidson, Donald. (1971). Agency. In A. R. N. Marras, R. Bronaugh, & R. W. Binkeley (Eds.), *Agent, Action, and Reason*. University of Toronto Press.

Davies, Mark. (2008–) The Corpus of Contemporary American English (COCA). Available online at http://corpus.byu.edu/coca/. Accessed 18/05/2020.

Davies, Mark. (2018) The iWeb Corpus. Available online at https://www.english-corpora.org/iWeb/. Accessed 18/05/2020.

Dik, Simon C. (1997). *The Theory of Functional Grammar: The structure of the clause* (K. Hengeveld (Ed.); second, revised). Berlin: Mouton de Gruyter.

Dowty, David. (1991). Thematic Proto-Roles and Argument Selection. *Language*, 67(3), 547–619.

Duranti, Alessandro. (2004). Agency in Language. In A. Duranti (Ed.), *A Companion to Linguistic Anthropology*. Malden: Blackwell Publishing.

Enfield, N. J. (2015). Linguistic Relativity from Reference to Agency. *Annual Review of Anthropology*, 44(1), 207–224.

Fanego, Teresa. (2018). A construction of independent means: The history of the Way construction revisited. *English Language and Linguistics*, 23(3), 671–699.

Ferretti, Gabriele, & Zipoli Caiani, Silvano. (2021). Habitual Actions, Propositional Knowledge, Motor Representations and Intentionality. *Topoi*, 1, 3, 623–635.

Gao, Tao, McCarthy, Gregory, & Scholl, Brian J. (2010). The wolfpack effect: Perception of animacy irresistibly influences interactive behavior. *Psychological Science*, 21(12), 1845–1853.

Gelman, Rochel, Durgin, Frank, & Kaufman, Lisa. (1995). Distinguishing between animates and inanimates: not by motion alone. In D. Sperberg, D. Premack, & A. J. Premack (Eds.), *Causal Cognition – A multidisciplinary debate* (pp. 150–184). New York: Clarendon Press.

Goldberg, Adele E. (1995). *A Construction Grammar Approach to Argument Structure*. Chicago: The University of Chicago Press.

Goldberg, Adele E. (2006). *Constructions at Work. The Nature of Generalization in Language*. Oxford: Oxford University Press.

Heider, Fritz, & Simmel, Marianne. (1944). An Experimental Study of Apparent Behavior. *The American Journal of Psychology*, 57(2), 259.

Hofrichter, Ruth, Mueller, Megan E., & Rutherford, M. D. (2021). Children's Perception of Animacy: Social Attributions to Moving Figures. *Perception*, 50(5), 387–398.

Israel, Michael. (1996). The way constructions grow. *Conceptual Structure, Discourse and Language*, 217, 217–230.

Jackendoff, Ray S. (1990). *Semantic Structures*. Cambridge (MA): The MIT press.

Ji, Jie, & Liang, Maocheng. (2018). An animacy hierarchy within inanimate nouns: English corpus evidence from a prototypical perspective. *Lingua*, 205, 71–89.

Lee, Su Mei, Gao, Tao, & McCarthy, Gregory. (2014). Attributing intentions to random motion engages the posterior superior temporal sulcus. *Social Cognitive and Affective Neuroscience*, 9(1), 81–87.

On Some Epistemic Access Effects

Francesco Costantini
University of Udine, Italy
francesco.costantini@uniud.it

Abstract

Recent research on subjunctive obviation, i.e. the unavailability of *de se* reading in (mostly) subjunctive clauses holding in a number of languages, has pointed out that obviation may depend on semantic and pragmatic constraints involving attitude predicates and the propositional content of the attitude itself. In line with this approach, the article explores the hypothesis whereby subjunctive obviation is related to the epistemic access to a propositional content. In particular I will discuss subjunctive obviation in Italian focusing on sentences involving doxastic attitude predicates in the first person. I will propose that subjunctive obviation is caused by a semantic clash arising when (i) the attitude predicate presupposes that the information conveyed in the embedded clause is epistemically accessed in an indirect way (by guessing, inferring, etc.) and (ii) the propositional content expressed in the embedded clause can only be accessed via introspection (i.e., it is object of "self-knowledge", as generally understood in the field of philosophy of language). This analysis accounts for the basic facts involving obviation in doxastic environments as well as novel data previously not reviewed; moreover, it suggests that the phenomenon is not limited to subjunctive clauses, but can also occur in indicative clauses, as long as a semantic clash arises between the attitude predicate semantics and the embedded clause semantics. While empirically limited to doxastic predicates, the present study may provide the founding for further analysis on obviation in other syntactic environments.

Keywords

obviation – doxastic predicates – epistemic access – evidentiality – self-knowledge

1 Introduction

The aim of the present article is showing that epistemic access can be called into play in order to account for a syntactic phenomenon that has puzzled linguists at least since the 1980s, namely subjunctive obviation. Broadly speaking subjunctive obviation refers to the unavailability of *de se* interpretation in subjunctive argument clauses in a number of languages, among which Romance languages (Bouchard 1984, Picallo 1985, Raposo 1985, Everaert 1986, Suñer 1986, Kempchinsky 1987, 1997, 2009, Rizzi 1991, Progovac 1993, 1994, Tsoulas 1996, Manzini 2000), Slavic languages (Avrutin 1994, Avrutin and Babyonyshev 1997, Szabolcsi 2010), Hungarian (Farkas 1992, Szabolcsi 2021) and Basque (Hornstein and San Martin 2001). Recent work on the phenomenon, mainly building on data from volitional predicates (Kaufmann 2019, 2020, Goncharov 2020; but see also Costantini 2016, Szabolcsi 2021 for other syntactic environments) has pointed to the fact that obviation may depend on semantic constraints involving attitude predicates and the propositional content of an attitude itself. In line with this approach to obviation, in the present paper I will return to a proposal I discussed in Costantini (2016), where focusing on the analysis of the phenomenon in clauses depending on doxastic predicates I explored the hypothesis whereby subjunctive obviation is related to the epistemic access to a propositional content. In doing this I will discuss subjunctive obviation in sentences involving *pensare* 'think' in the first person singular as the main verb (although other attitude predicates, such *credere* 'believe', *supporre* 'suppose, guess', *temere* 'be afraid, suspect', *sperare* 'hope', behave similarly, see Costantini 2010 and above mentioned literature). The basic idea that I will explore (in informal terms) is that subjunctive obviation obtains when a semantic clash arises between an attitude predicate presupposing that the information conveyed in the embedded clause is indirectly accessed and the propositional content expressed in the embedded clause, which is instead introspectively accessible (that is, it is object of "self-knowledge", as generally understood in the field of philosophy of language and philosophy of mind, see Shoemaker 1996, Burge 1988, 1996, 2007, Recanati 2007). It follows from this that "subjunctive" obviation is not limited to subjunctive clauses, but can also result in indicative clauses (as empirically pointed out in Szabolcsi 2021 for Hungarian) as long as a semantic clash between the attitude predicate semantics and the embedded clause semantics arises. Moreover, I show that the analysis discussed here accounts for unrelated phenomena which were not previously discussed in relation with subjunctive obviation, providing independent support for the proposed hypothesis; thus, while empirically limited to one doxastic predicate only, the present contribution may provide the founding for analysis on obviation even in other syntactic environments.

The paper is organized as follows: in section 2 I discuss the empirical framework concerning obviation in doxastic attitude reports in Italian; In section 3 I provide an interpretation of the data and discuss the machinery needed to reach the relevant generalizations; moreover, I discuss in more detail the interpretation the relevant sentences in section 2 have and show that obviative attitude reports appear to involve a specific way of epistemic access to information, namely introspection, vis-à-vis nonobviative attitude reports. In section 4 I propose a hypothesis and show how it accounts for the data in section 2. In section 5 I discuss some related phenomena and show they are directly derivable from the hypothesis discussed here. Section 6 concludes the article.

2 Subjunctive Obviation

It is a well-known fact that in some languages the subject of an embedded clause in the subjunctive receives an obviative interpretation with respect to the matrix subject. In Italian, for instance, sentence (1) is infelicitous because the matrix subject and the embedded subject refer to the same individual.

(1) # Penso   che   io   parta   domani
    think-1SG   that   I   leave-SUBJ.PRES.1SG   tomorrow
    Lit. 'I think that I leave tomorrow.'

Sentence (1) minimally contrasts with example (2), which shows that the sentence is acceptable if the matrix subject and the embedded subject are not coreferential.

(2) Penso   che   Ø   parta   domani
    think-1SG   that   Ø   leave-SUBJ.PRES.3SG   tomorrow
    'I think he/she is/is going to/will leave tomorrow.'

Sentence (1) also minimally contrasts with sentence (3) and (4).

(3) Penso   che   Ø   partirò   domani
    think-1SG   that   Ø   leave-IND.FUT-1SG   tomorrow
    'I think I'll leave tomorrow.'

(4) Penso   di   PRO partire   domani
    think-1SG   C   PRO leave-INF   tomorrow
    'I think I'll leave tomorrow.'

Sentence (3) shows (or at least *seems* to show, as it would become apparent later on; see also Szabolcsi 2021) that the obviative interpretation of the embedded subject with respect to the matrix subject only concerns subjunctive clauses.

Sentence (4) contrasts with (1) in that infinitival clauses can only trigger a coreferential reading between the matrix subject and PRO.

The phenomenon appears to be particularly puzzling because as originally discussed in Ruwet (1984) not all subjunctive clauses have been shown to be obviative. Ruwet notices that the type of predicate, as well as tense, aspect and voice of the embedded verb appear to improve the acceptability of sentences where the matrix subject and the embedded subject refer to the same individual, so that the obviative interpretation is someway weakened. For instance, sentence (5), where the embedded verb in the subjunctive is modal, is intuitively acceptable.

(5) Penso   che io possa   partire   domani
    think-1SG that I   can-SUBJ.PRES.1SG   leave-INF tomorrow
    'I think I can leave tomorrow.'

Similarly, sentence (6), where the embedded verb is in the past subjunctive, appears to be acceptable, too (or at least not as unacceptable as sentence (1)).

(6) Penso   che io abbia   fatto molti errori
    think-1SG that I   have.SUBJ.PRES.1SG   made   many mistakes
    'I think I have made many mistakes.'

Similarly, sentence (7), where the embedded verb is (past) passive, is also acceptable for most Italian speakers.

(7) Penso   che io sia   stato ingannato
    think-1SG that I   be.SUBJ.PRES.1SG   been   cheated
    'I think I've been cheated.'

How exactly the features of the embedded predicate affect the acceptability of sentences like (1) on one hand and (4), (5) and (6) on the other has been object of extensive investigation (see Costantini 2010 for a discussion on the main proposals) but is still an open question.

3   Obviation and *de se* Attitude Reports

A promising way to tackle the question seems to me Ruwet's (1984), Farkas (1992) and Schlenker's (2005) observation whereby the different status of sentence (1) as opposed to (4), (5) and (6) does not involve the interpretation of the matrix and embedded subjects only, but lays in the different semantic import conveyed by the embedded clause as a whole. Ruwet (1984), for instance, suggests that sentences where the embedded subject receives an obviative interpretation convey a "discontinuity" between and the attitude expressed in the matrix clause (specifically, will, as Ruwet's article focuses on French *vouloir* 'want') and the capability on the part of the individual the embedded subject refers to perform the action the embedded verb expresses. Farkas (1992) suggests that her notion of "responsibility" (Farkas 1988) may discriminate between sentences like (1) on one hand and sentences like (5) and (6) on the other (sentences like (7) are not explicitly addressed in her article). Finally, Schlenker (2005) captures the different status of sentences (1) vs (5), (6) and (7) by suggesting that the situation denoted in sentence (1) as opposed to (5), (6) and (7) involves a specific type of interpretation (called "event-*de se*" interpretation), which can only be expressed through an infinitive structure (see (4)). As this latter point seems to me particularly promising for the analysis, as it will become evident soon, I will look at it in some more detail by clarifying the idea of *de se* interpretation and of "event-*de se*" interpretation.

In his seminal work on the interpretation that was later labelled "*de se*" (Lewis 1979), Castañeda (1968: 449) illustrates the basic idea through the following story: "A man, to be called 'Quintus', is brought unconscious to a military tent, but on gaining consciousness suffers from amnesia, and during the next months becomes a war hero and gets lost in combat and completely forgets the military chapter of his life. Later on Quintus studies all accounts of the war hero". While he is not aware he is actually reading about himself, in such a scenario Quintus could not possibly utter a sentence like (8) (assuming he is an Italian speaker!); sentence (9) would instead be felicitous.

(8) # *Sono un eroe!*
    # I am a hero!

(9) *Quest'uomo è un eroe!*
    This man is a hero!

If now someone reported Quintus' thinking, she would not utter the sentence in (10), while (11) would be acceptable.

(10) *Quintus   pensa   di   essere   un   eroe*
     Quintus   thinks   C   be-INF   a   hero
     'Quintus believes himself to be a hero'.

(11) | *Quintus* | *pensa* | *che* | *lui* | *sia* | | *un* | *eroe*
| Quintus | thinks | that | he | be.SUBJ.PRES.3SG | | a | hero

'Quintus thinks he is a hero'.

Now, sentence (10) exemplifies an attitude *de se*, that is, an attitude about the attitude holder herself (Pearson's 2016 "aboutness condition") and for which the attitude holder is aware that the attitude is about herself (Pearson's 2016 "awareness condition"): in other words, (10) is only acceptable in a scenario whereby Quintus is aware the person he is reading about is himself and is thinking about himself as a hero. Sentence (11), on the other hand, exemplifies a non-*de se* attitude, as the attitude holder is not aware he is thinking about himself.

Let us now get back to obviation and to do so let us make an addition to Castañeda's story. Let us now suppose that after reading about the deeds of the war hero (who is in fact himself) Quintus starts realizing from what he has been told about his past that the person he is reading about may be himself. He then may utter:

(12) | *Comincio* | *a* | *pensare* | *che* | *io* | *sia* | | *un* | *eroe*
| start-1SG | P | think | that | I | be.SUBJ.PRES.3SG | | a | hero

'I'm starting to think that I'm a hero.'

Notice that the sentence is natural despite the matrix and the embedded subjects are both first person pronouns and the embedded clause is in the subjunctive. Thus sentence (12) does not involve subjunctive obviation and is on a par with sentences (5), (6) and (7). Notice also that the attitude report in (12) is *de se*, as both Pearsons's (2016) "aboutness" and the "awareness" conditions appear to be satisfied.

Moreover, one has to notice that while sentence (12) expresses a *de se* attitude, the belief expressed in the sentence expresses a self-ascription of a property as based on "demonstration" (Pryor 1999) and not on memory, perception, or general knowledge about oneself, that is, on introspection. Proof of it is that the use of the first person as subject is here not immune to error through misidentification (Shoemaker 1968). It may well be the case that in the scenario described above the amnesiac misjudges what he is reading and that after all the war hero he is reading about is not actually himself.

All of this of course calls into question the epistemic access to information. Schlenker's (2006) idea of "event *de se*", if I interpret it correctly, seems to refer exactly to the way information about oneself is achieved. "Event *de se*" attitudes can be understood as attitudes towards propositions accessed via introspection; "non-event *de se*" attitudes as attitudes towards propositions differently accessed (though report, hearsay, inference, etc.). To illustrate, I mention here the discussion on *remember* (and *imagine*) in Higginbotham (2003), which is also mentioned by Schlenker in defining the notion of event-*de se*. Higginbotham shows that gerundive complements of the verbs *remember* and *imagine* are to be distinguished from *that*-clauses. Consider for instance sentences (13) and (14):

(13) I remember that my grandfather was called "Rufus".

(14) I remember my grandfather being called "Rufus".

These sentences have different truth conditions: Imagine the speaker's grandfather died before she was born; under this circumstance sentence (13) would be acceptable, sentence (14) would be false. In sentence (14), but not in sentence (13), the embedded event has an "internal" (introspective) epistemic access. Apparently Schlenker's notion of "event *de se*" refers exactly to this type of epistemic access, that is, introspection.

Let us now depart from Schlenker's theory of obviation and let us delve into epistemic access and how it relates to obviation. To start with, let us consider the properties of introspective epistemic access and more precisely on the related notion of "self-knowledge", as used in philosophy of language and philosophy of mind. Self-knowledge (or "self-consciousness", "self-awareness" as it is sometimes referred to) is meant as the knowledge of one's own mental states, such as beliefs, wishes, emotions, sensations, etc. (Shoemaker 1996, Burge 1988, 1996, 2007, Recanati 2007. See Gertler 2011 for an outlook on the main questions concerning self-knowledge).

Self-knowledge has been viewed as something different from knowledge about the world "external" to oneself. First, it relies on a unique method of knowledge, that is, introspection. Introspection lets one have a direct access to mental states and is highly epistemically secure. Because of this, if a speaker utters sentence (15)a, it would be nonsensical to ask the question in (15)b.

(15) a.   I feel pain
    b. #   How do you know?

By contrast, this question is not odd if the speaker utters sentence (16)a, which of course does not involve introspective knowledge, since one may question the source of knowledge and the reliability of information about someone else.

(16) a. He feels pain
     b. How do you know?

Second, in self-ascribing a mental state, the subject is authoritative, that is, under normal circumstances self-knowledge is endowed with the presumption of truth. Thus, if the speaker utters sentence (17)a, challenging the statement by uttering (17)b is normally infelicitous ((17)b would be acceptable only if the speaker was implying that the interlocutor was lying or she was questioning the interlocutor's standards related to pain perception).

(17) a.   I feel pain
     b. # No, you don't!

By contrast, replying through (18)b to the sentence in (18)a may be appropriate.

(18) a. He feels pain
     b. No, he doesn't!

From a morphosyntactic viewpoint the notion of self-knowledge can be linked to different modes of evidentiality, the grammatical category indicating the source and the reliability of information (Chafe and Nichols 1986), such as "direct" evidentiality (Willett 1988, Faller 2011, 2020, Davis et al. 2007), "ego-evidentiality" (Garrett 2001) or "egophoric" evidentiality (Bergqvist, Kittilä 2020: 2; on egophoricity see also Hargreaves 2005, Speas et al. 2013, Bergqvist, Kittilä 2017), or, again, "general knowledge" (Kittilä 2019). By "direct" information it is generally meant information based first-hand on visual or auditory evidence (see Aikhenvald 2004: 43); by "egophoricity" it is generally meant the grammatical category expressing information accessible to the speaker as personal knowledge or general knowledge, that is knowledge that has become part of the internal information of the speaker, of which she has absolute certainty and does not need any kind of external evidence (Kittilä 2019: 1275). While some languages have specific morphological markers encoding the source of information, some others do not (see Higginbotham 2009 for a discussion on the relevance of the notion of evidentiality for languages who do not encode it morphologically). For instance in Central Pomo specific morphemes encode whether the information expressed in a proposition is based on general knowledge, visual evidence, auditory evidence, report or inference (Kittilä 2019):

(19) a. čh é mul=ʔma
         rain-fall=GEN
         'It rained' (as an established fact)
    b.   čh é mul=ya
         rain-fall=VIS
         'I saw it rained'
    c.   čh é mul=ʔdo
         rain-fall=REP
         'I was told it rained'
    d.   čh é mul=nme
         rain-fall=AUD
         'I heard it rained'
    e.   čh é mul=ʔka
         rain fall=INFR
         'It must have rained'

Italian – as well as other Romance languages – does not have specific evidential morphology but resorts to "evidentiality strategies" (Squartini 2001, 2008, 2018) to express the source of information. Thus, for instance, in Italian the imperfect and the future tense as well as the conditional mood have evidential uses. The conditional mood can be used to express hearsay or unconfirmed information, as in the following example:

(20) *Secondo   le   ultime   informazioni il   presidente   avrebbe*
     According-to the   latest   information the   president   have.COND
     lasciato   Roma   ieri
     left   Rome   yesterday
     'According to the latest information the president left Rome yesterday.'

Among the evidential strategies available in Italian, following Izvorski (1997), Simons (2008), and Squartini (2018) (see also Mari and Portner 2021) I assume that doxastic predicates, like *believe, think, guess, suppose,* etc. can function as indirect or inferential evidentials. The sentence in (21), for instance, indicates that the information expressed in the embedded clause is not completely reliable and the source of the information is not the speaker's own perceptual experience, as the literature on epistemic modality has extensively shown (see von Fintel and Gillies 2010, Mari 2016, Giannikidou and Mari 2016).

(21) *Penso   stia   piovendo*
     think-1SG   AUX.SUBJ.PRES.3SG   raining
     'I think it's raining.'

This sentence would not be felicitous in a scenario where, for instance, the speaker is seeing from her window that it is raining, or where she is walking in the rain. In a scenario where a speaker perceives that it is raining (assuming she is not experiencing some sort of delusion), a sentence like (22) might instead be uttered.

(22) Sta   piovendo
      AUX-IND.PRES.3SG   raining
      'It's raining.'

These observations suggest that introspective information cannot be embedded under doxastic predicates exactly because of a clash between evidential sources: doxastic predicates introduce the information expressed in the embedded clause either as not reliable (to different extents) or as indirect or inferred; on the contrary, proposition based on introspection are truthful.

One may reach the same conclusion by calling on the notion of clausal implicature as defined in Gazdar (1979: 57ss.) and Levinson (1982: 136–137), who point out that belief verbs introduce clausal implicatures as in (23).

(23) Clausal implicature Levinson (1982: 136)
      If S asserts some complex expression p which (i) contains an embedded sentence q, and (ii) p neither entails nor presupposes q and (iii) there's an alternative expression r of roughly equal brevity which contains q such that r *does* entail or presupposes q; *then*, by asserting p rather than r, S implicates that he doesn't know whether q is true or false, i.e. he implicates Pp & $P \sim q$.

The basic intuition behind the idea of clausal implicature is that if a linguistic expression fails to commit the speaker to a proposition as compared to a linguistic expression that commits the speaker to a proposition, this may be taken to implicate that the speaker is not in an epistemic position to accept the stronger alternative. Thus, if I utter the sentence *I think it is raining* instead of *It is raining* I implicate that I do not know whether it is raining and for all I know it may not be raining. Moreover, a sentence like *I think it is raining* would be infelicitous in a context where I am quite aware that it is raining.[1]

---

[1] For a discussion on a related topic, see Chemla (2008). I thank an anonymous reviewer for raising this point.

4   Epistemic Access as Source of Obviation

Turning now back to obviation, these observations suggest that the status of sentences like (1) as opposed to (5), (6) and (7) may derive from a clash between the semantics of doxastic predicates as a strategy to express indirect evidence and the semantics of the embedded clause as expression of self-knowledge (introspective, directly accessible, non-inferential knowledge). We may then formulate the following hypothesis:

(24) A syntactic structure α v φ is obviative, if
   (i)   v is a predicate implying an indirect access to a proposition, and
   (ii) φ is a proposition accessible through introspection.

Notice that under (24) obviation is not constrained by mood – that is, (24) predicts that obviation can occur in subjunctive clauses as well as in indicative clauses as long as the matrix verb implies an indirect access to the embedded proposition and the proposition is accessed via introspection. Thus, 'subjunctive obviation' is not in fact related to subjunctive mood, as in fact already shown in Szabolcsi (2021), but is an instantiation of a more general set of phenomena involving epistemic access. I will return to this point in the following section. Before addressing this point I will implement the hypothesis in (24) and show how it accounts for the data illustrated in section 2.

Let us first consider sentences like (1) in view of (24). One can notice that in sentence (1), the embedded eventuality most naturally refers to a future time reference, although no future morphology occurs. This suggests that the embedded clause is futurate, that is, "a sentence with no obvious means of future reference, which nonetheless conveys that a future oriented eventuality is planned, scheduled, or otherwise determined" (Copley 2008; for a similar idea on subjunctive see Mari 2016: 67–68). Copley (2008) shows that futurates assert the existence of a plan such that an entity (the "director", as she dubs it) has the desire for the plan to be realized and is committed to carry out the plan. Moreover, futurates presuppose that the director has the ability to act to the effect that the plan is realized.

Quite obviously, plans are mental states, which, as such, can be accessed via introspection in the normal case: One is normally aware of one's own plans and applying the diagnostics in (15)–(18) easily shows this point: It is pointless to question the source of a sentence like (25)a, as in (25)b.

(25) a.   *Domani*   *vado*   *dal*   *dottore*
          Tomorrow   go.IND.PRES-1SG   to-the   doctor
          'I'm going to the doctor's tomorrow.'

b. # Come   lo   sai?
     How   it   know-2SG
     'How do you know that?'

Copley also points out that the director may be determined contextually or may be accommodated (Copley 2008: 270). In sentence (26), for instance, the presupposed director corresponds by default to the speaker, but it may also be someone else who is in the position to devise the speaker's leaving (for instance a superior in a workplace).

(26) *Parto*   *domani*
     leave-IND.PRES.1SG   tomorrow
     I'm leaving tomorrow.

As for embedded clauses, the director in a futurate sentence can also correspond to the subject, it can be established contextually, or it can be accommodated. Thus, in a sentence like (27), the hearer's leaving may be planned by the hearer herself or by another contextually relevant individual.

(27) *Mi*   *hanno*   *detto*   *che*   *parti*   *domani.*
     1SG.DAT   have-3PL   told   that   leave-IND.PRES.2SG   tomorrow
     'They told me you are leaving tomorrow.'

Let us now turn to sentence (1). The embedded clause in (1) seems to be futurate, as it has a *present* subjunctive morphology but refers to a future event. Thus, it involves a plan and asserts the existence of an individual, a 'director', conceiving the plan and having the desire for it to be brought about. Now, let us suppose that in sentence (1) the director corresponds to the subject of the embedded clause, so that the sentence expresses a self-ascription of a plan. It follows that since doxastic predicates function as indirect evidentials, the sentence indicates that the information conveyed in the embedded clause is *not* epistemically reliable from the point of view of the attitude holder (which in this case coincides with the speaker). Because self-ascribing a plan involves introspection, a semantic clash arises because of the indirect evidential nature expressed by the matrix predicate and the introspective nature of the self-ascription of a mental state. It follows that the propositional attitude in (1) cannot be *de se*.[2]

---

2   An anonymous reviewer suggests that a sentence like (i) is predicted to be acceptable, contrary to facts, because access to the embedded propositional content is not introspective.
    (i) # *Credo che io la convinca.*
           'I think I convince (subj) her.'

The same conclusion can be reached by resorting to the notion of clausal implicature. By (23), (1) implicates that the subject of the attitude does not know that she herself, qua the subject of the attitude, is committed to a plan and that for all she knows, it may be the case that she has no plans at all. But this is of course nonsensical, because the epistemic access to one's own plans is introspective. Thus, again, the propositional attitude in (1) cannot be *de se*.

Notice that the same reasoning does not hold true for sentences like (3), where the embedded verb has future morphology. Future predicates do not typically express plans, but rather predictions or expectations, which are independent from one's plans (see Copley 2006; see also Mari 2014 and Mari and Portner 2021). Thus, asserting (28) is infelicitous because the event is unplannable (excluding the scenario where the match result is fixed), whereas (29) is acceptable.

(28) # La   Francia vince   i   mondiali
     The   France   win-IND.PRES.3SG   the world championship

(29) La   Francia vincerà   i   mondiali
     The   France   win-IND.FUT.3SG   the world championship
     'France will win the world championship.'

As future morphology does not presuppose the existence of a plan, introspection is not at issue in sentences where the embedded verb is in the future indicative, so that (24) does not rule out (3).

Let us now consider the cases of "obviation weakening" (sentences (5), (6) and (7)). The hypothesis pursued here predicts that obviation obtains if and only if the embedded clause expresses a propositional content accessible via introspection. If the hypothesis is correct, we expect that in examples (5), (6) and (7) the propositional content does not involve introspective access to information. In what follows I show that this appears to be the case.

Let us consider first example (5), where an epistemic modal occurs in the embedded clause. The fact that one can reply as in (30)b to sentence (30)a shows that this type of modality does not express introspective knowledge.

(30) a.   I may have made many mistakes.
     b.   How do you know that?

Thus, the fact that obviation does not occur in sentence (5) is expected.

I claim that the propositional content is in fact introspectively accessed as long as it expresses a plan on the part of the speaker.

The same reasoning can be applied to sentence (6). Remember that past eventualities can be recollected introspectively, through one's own memory ("from the inside" in Pryor and Higginbotham sense) or by demonstration. Remembering "from the inside" is clearly introspective and one would expect that a doxastic attitude towards a past eventuality cannot be *de se* in this case. This appears to be obviously correct. Imagine that I have just eaten an ice-cream. I could not reasonably utter sentence (31) (unless I suffer from short term memory loss), which does instantiate an obviative interpretation.³

(31) # *Penso   che   io   abbia   appena mangiato un*
      Think-1SG that   I   have.SUBJ.PRES1SG   just   eaten   an
      gelato
      ice-cream
      'I think I've just eaten an ice-cream.'

However, if one remembers a past eventuality involving oneself by recollecting some circumstances in one's own past, that is, by demonstration, one expects that obviation will not occur. This also appears to be correct. Suppose that I am talking about my first school day. I do not remember how I went to school on that precise day, but I remember that I used to go to school by car during my years as a schoolboy. In this scenario answer (32)b to question (32)a appears to be acceptable.

(32) a. *Come sei   andato   a   scuola   il   primo   giorno?*
        How   be.2SG   gone   to   school   the first   day
        'How did you go to school on your first school day?'

     b. *Penso   che   io   ci   sia   andato   in auto*
        think-1SG that   I   there be.SUBJ.PRES.1SG gone   in car
        'I think I went by car.'

The status of sentence (5) can be derived in the same way. The sentence is felicitous only in a scenario where the speaker has not yet come to know – that is, she is unaware, she has no introspective knowledge – that she has made mistakes.

---

3 An anonymous reviewer points out that even assuming a scenario where sentence (31) would be acceptable, a contrast is intuitively perceivable between (31) and a sentence like (37). I assume that this may be due to the semantics of lexical units included in the latter sentence, which entail an indirect access to the propositional content.

Finally, let us consider sentence (6). Applying the diagnostics in (14)–(17) to the embedded clause in (6), it can be shown that the content (apart from referring to a past eventuality) is clearly *not* accessible through introspection. One can indeed reply as in (33)b to sentence (33)a.

(33) a. I've been cheated.
     b. How do you know that?

Hence, since the embedded clause does not express introspective knowledge, the obviative interpretation is also predicted not to occur.

5 Other Expected Outcomes

Let us consider now what predictions emerge from the hypothesis explored here.

First, let us observe that while sentence (1) involves a futurate embedded clause, the analysis discussed here does not require that the embedded clause must be futurate. Obviation is predicted to obtain whenever the propositional content introduced in the embedded clause is accessible through introspection, be it future-oriented or not. At least three examples of sentences corresponding to this description comes to one's mind.

The first involves embedded clauses that express the self-ascription of sensations and mental state, which by definitions are accessible through introspection. Thus, for instance, feeling ill or dizzy or sad is normally a matter of introspective knowledge. As expected, a sentence like (34) results odd, unless the nature itself of the physical state the attitude holder is self-ascribing is in question.[4]

(34) # *Penso   che io stia   male*
       think-1SG that I   stay-SUBJ.PRES.1SG   bad
       'I think I'm feeling sick.'

---

[4] An anonymous reviewer points out that the sentence (i) sounds acceptable despite one presumably has access on whether one is falling in love:
(i) *Credo che io mi stia (subj) innamorando*
    'I think I'm falling in love'.
I assume that the more natural scenario where the sentence is interpretable is one where the speaker is not sure whether what she is feeling can be defined as 'falling in love' (as compared to just 'liking' someone); thus introspective access concerns one's own feeling but not their definition in terms of 'falling in love'. The case is similar to sentence (34), which may be acceptable in a situation where the speaker is not completely assured that what she is feeling is pain or just discomfort.

A second example concerns progressive eventualities. In the normal case someone is aware about what she is voluntarily doing. The diagnostics in (14)–(17) clearly shows that (35)a, which includes a progressive eventuality, involves introspective knowledge, as it would be odd to question it, as in (35)b.

(35) a. I'm reading the newspaper.
　　 b. # How do you know that?

As expected, when the embedded clause includes a progressive periphrasis involving the attitude bearer as an aware agent, obviation arises, as in (36).

(36) # *Penso　che io stia　　　　　　leggendo il　giornale*
　　　 think-1SG that I AUX-SUBJ.PRES.1SG reading　the newspaper
　　　 'I think I'm reading the newspaper.'

If however the embedded clause including a progressive does not imply an introspective access to information, it is expected that the obviative interpretation does not obtain. This appears to be correct, as shown in the following example:

(37) *Penso　che io stia　　　　　　scrivendo alla　persona sbagliata*
　　　 think-1SG that I AUX-SUBJ.PRES.1SG reading　to-the wrong　person
　　　 'I think I'm writing to the wrong person.'

Third, habitual eventualities are also intuitively liable to involve introspective knowledge, as is shown in (37). Notice that this type of eventuality typically involve ego-evidential morphology in languages that use it (see Kittilä 2019).

(38) a. I read the newspaper every morning.
　　 b. # How do you know that?

Thus, obviation is predicted to arise if the embedded clause includes a habitual predicate, as in sentence (39).

(39) # *Penso　che io legga　　　　　il　giornale　ogni mattina*
　　　 think-1SG that I read-SUBJ.PRES.1SG the newspaper every morning
　　　 'I think I read the newspaper every morning.'

Another consequence of the proposal discussed here is that obviation may occur no matter what the mood selected by the main predicate is (not only in subjunctive clause), as long as a semantic clash occurs between the implicatures the sentence introduces and the semantic import of the embedded clause. To test whether this prediction is correct let us consider semifactive verbs in Italian (e.g. *sapere* 'know', *scoprire* 'discover'), which typically select for indicative embedded clauses.[5]

(40) Ho   saputo che Maria è   partita
     have.1SG known   that Maria be-IND.PRES.1SG left
     'I have come to know that Maria has left.'

In using these verbs, one implicates that the source of information is indirect. Sentence (40), for instance, is normally infelicitous in a context where the speaker has witnessed Maria's leaving. Thus, if the embedded clause expresses a proposition whose source can only be introspection, obviation is expected to occur under the hypothesis discussed here. Example (41)–(43), where the same predicates occur in the embedded clause as in (35), (36) and (37), show that this prediction is correct.

(41) # Ho   saputo   che   sto   male
       have-1SG known   that AUX-IND.PRES.1SG bad
       'I've come to know that I'm feeling sick.'

(42) # Ho   saputo che   sto   leggendo il giornale
       have-1SG known   that AUX-IND.PRES.1SG reading   the newspaper
       'I've come to know that I'm reading the newspaper.'

---

5 A subjunctive verb can occur in a clause selected by a semifactive verb only if the negation cooccurs, as in (i):
(i) *Non so se Maria sia partita.*
   'I don't know whether Maria is(subj) left'.
In the following examples the matrix verb is in the present perfect (*passato prossimo*) in order to facilitate the desired reading, where the focus is on the information conveyed in the embedded clause and not on the attitude predicate. As an anonymous reviewer points out, the present tense of 'know' can be combined with a proposition like 'I feel sick':
(ii) *So che sto male.*
   'I know I feel sick.'
While the sentence is acceptable when high pitch intonation aligns with the matrix verb, the sentence is odd if uttered with a plain intonation. Thus, the status of sentences (41)–(43) does not depend on the tense/aspect of the main verb.

(43) # Ho   saputo   che leggo   il giornale ogni
     have-1SG known   that read-IND.PRES.1SG the newspaper every
     mattina
     morning
     'I've come to know that read the newspaper every morning.'

But if the embedded predicate implies an indirectly accessible information, then again a perfectly natural sentence obtains. Thus it is possible to build a parallel of (37) using a semifactive verb in the main clause, as is shown in (44).

(44) Ho   capito   che   sto   scrivendo alla
     have-1SG understood that stay-IND.PRES.1SG reading   to-the
     persona   sbagliata
     wrong   person
     'I've realized that I'm writing to the wrong person.'

6   Alternative Analyses

Some previous analyses on obviation have associated the phenomenon with the availability of an infinitival clause expressing a nonobviative meaning in the same syntactic environments where subjunctive triggers the obviative interpretation (Farkas 1992, Schlenker 2005; see also Bouchard 1983 and Costantini 2013, who investigates obviation in relative and adverbial clauses w.r.t. mood competition). Farkas (1992) claims that subjunctive obviation is determined by a semantic principle requiring that the infinitive blocks the subjunctive in what she calls "canonical control cases", that is, environments where an argument of the matrix predicate can control PRO, and where the embedded subject is in a responsibility relation ("RESP") with the embedded eventuality – where by "responsibility relation" is meant the relation "between an individual and a situation if the individual brings the situation about" (see also Farkas 1988). In the same spirit, Schlenker (2005) resorts to infinitive-subjunctive mood competition, although he revises Farkas's original mechanism by introducing the divide between individual and event *de se*, as mentioned above, and deriving obviation from two pragmatic principles, *Maximize presupposition!*, and *Prefer de se!*

(45) *Maximize presupposition!* (Heim 1991, Sauerland 2003)
     The strongest possible presupposition must be marked on variables.

(46) *Prefer de se!*
A *de se* logical form should be preferred over a *de re* logical form whenever this is compatible with the situation which is reported.

Principle (45) has the effect that linguistic expressions that introduce a presupposition should be preferred to linguistic expressions that do not, which are consequently "semantic default" expressions. Schlenker claims that infinitival clauses carry the presupposition that the attitude is *de se*, whereas the subjunctive is a default mood and does not introduce presuppositions (mainly because its use does not seem to be compatible with a consistent semantics). Hence, he proposes that, as a result of the principles in (45) and (46), "when an embedded clause is intended as being *de se* both with respect to the subject and with respect to the event argument of the embedded verb, the infinitival should be preferred to the subjunctive clause, and that in other cases the subjunctive should be admissible".

It has already been noticed in the literature (see Szabolcsi 2021 w.r.t Hungarian) that in some examples obviation obtains (i) in indicative argument clauses and (ii) despite no infinitival competitor occurs. She discusses examples like the following ones, where the embedded verb is in the indicative and no infinitival competitor is available due to the main verb selectional restrictions (Szabolci's examples (20)e, f, g):

(47) # *Remélem, hogy fél lábon állok*
       hope-1SG that   stay-1SG
       'I hope that I'm standing on one leg'

(48) # *Remélem, hogy (nem) szédülök*
       hope-1SG that (not) have-vertigo-1SG
       'I hope that I (don't) have vertigo'

(49) # *Remélem, hogy (nem) fázom*
       hope-1SG that (not) have-cold-1SG
       'I hope that that I'm (not) cold'

One can easily notice that the three examples, which convey what Szabolcsi calls "mind boggling meanings" are in fact very similar in nature to some of the Italian examples discussed above in that the embedded clause expresses information that is normally accessed to by introspection.

Thus, apparently obviation is only instantiated by semantic and pragmatic constraints and not by syntactic constraints.

If the analysis I have explored here is correct, it is also expected that epistemic access effects holds in a number of other cases where no mood competition is involved. I will discuss here a couple of issues that may be easily handled with in view of the hypothesis discussed here and marginally involve obviation as well (though not in the exact phenomenology traditionally discussed in the literature on subjunctive obviation).

First, consider again example (36). Mood competition hypotheses predict that an infinitival competitor must rule out the sentence in the subjunctive; this is however contrary to fact due to morphosyntactic restrictions in Italian preventing the progressive periphrasis (the auxiliary *stare* 'stay' followed by a verb in the gerund) to occur in the infinitive (see ex. (50)).[6]

(50) # Penso   di   star   leggendo il   giornale
     think-1SG C   AUX-SUBJ.PRES.1SG reading   the newspaper
     'I think I'm reading the newspaper.'

Thus, sentence in (36) is unacceptable even though a competing sentence having the infinitive embedded clause is unavailable. On the other hand, the idea that obviation follows from a semantic clash accounts for the status of (36) straightforwardly.

The second case I would like to draw attention on concerns epistemic modals. Epistemic modals have three properties: First, they cannot select for a control infinitival argument clause (Epstein 1984, Bhatt and Izvorski 1998).

(51) * È   probabile   leggere   il   giornale
       is probable   read-INF   the newspaper

Second, in Italian epistemic predicates select for subjunctive clauses.

(52) È   probabile   che   piova
     is probable   that   rain-SUBJ.PRES.3SG
     'It is probable it will rain'

Third, epistemic predicates introduce an implicit argument – "judge", as Lasersohn (2005) dubs it – in view of whose evidence an epistemic possibility or necessity is asserted. If not differently specified, the judge argument is satisfied by the speaker coordinates (see Lasersohn 2005).

Epistemic modals are clearly uttered in view of some indirect evidence; the proposition under epistemic modality cannot express direct knowledge

---

6 I thank an anonymous reviewer for directing my attention to the example.

(see Karttunen 1979, von Fintel and Gillies 2010, Giannikidou and Mari 2016, Goodhue 2017: remember that direct knowledge – that is, knowledge based on one's own sensory perceptions – is itself object of self-knowledge as defined above). For instance sentence (52) would be infelicitous if uttered by an individual walking in the rain or watching from a window the rain pouring. According to the hypothesis discussed here, a proposition expressing self-knowledge cannot be embedded under an epistemic modal, which seems to be correct in view of examples like the following one:

(53) # *È probabile che io stia leggendo il giornale.*
    lit. 'It is probable that I am reading the newspaper.'

Notice that since epistemic modals cannot select for infinitival clauses, sentence (53) should in principle not be odd, at least assuming a strong interpretation of the infinitive-subjunctive competition. Of course it is open to question whether this specific environment is genuine with respect to the discussion on obviation, but if the judge argument can be interpreted as encoded syntactically, nothing prevents to treat sentences including an epistemic modal on a par with sentences like (1). In any case, the status of example (53) follows straightforwardly from the hypothesis pursued here.[7]

A second case where the hypothesis pursued here seems to work correctly vis-à-vis mood competition theories of obviation involves psych-verbs and control. Let us start from two observations: First, in Italian some psych-verbs, e.g. *piacere* 'please', select an oblique experiencer (see Belletti and Rizzi 1988).

(54) *Mi   piace   questo*
    1sg.DAT likes   this
    'I like this' (lit. 'this likes to me')

Second, in infinitival clauses PRO can only be a canonical subject (compare examples (55)a and (55)b) and cannot be an oblique DP (see example (56)a and (56)b).

---

7   An anonymous reviewer points out that although both belief predicates and *probable* are incompatible with direct evidence, still there is a contrast between sentence (1) and the following:
   (i) *È probabile che io parta domani.*
       'It is probable that I leave(subj) tomorrow'.
   It is my intuition that that sentence (i) can only be acceptable under the interpretation whereby the 'director' of the plan expressed in the embedded clause is not the speaker herself. The sentence would be unacceptable if the 'director' coincided with the speaker.

(55) a. *Pietro   teme   questo*
    Pietro   fears   this
    'Pietro is afraid of this'

b. *Pietro   ha   detto   di   PRO   temere   questo*
    Pietro   has   said   C   PRO   fear-INF   this
    'Pietro has said he's afraid of this' (lit. 'Pietro has said to be afraid of this)

(56) a. *A   Pietro   piace   questo*
    to   Pietro   likes   this
    'Pietro likes this' (lit. 'This likes to Pietro')

b. * *Pietro   ha   detto   di   PRO   piacere   questo*
    Pietro   has   said   C   PRO   like-INF   this

Now, it is possible to build examples where the embedded clause in the subjunctive contains a psych-verb selecting for an oblique experiencer. Since clauses including psych-verbs typically express mental states, self-ascribing a proposition involving this type of predicates expresses self-knowledge, as example (57) shows – it is nonsensical to reply to sentence (57)a through sentence (57)b, exactly because the former sentence builds on introspection.

(57) a.   I like ice-cream
    b. # How do you know that?

Hence, the hypothesis explored here predicts that sentences having a doxastic predicate as its main verb and an embedded clause including a psych-verb and an oblique experiencer referring to the bearer of the attitude should be odd. This prediction seems to be correct in view of the following example:

(58) # *Penso   che   mi   piaccia   il   gelato*
    think-1SG   that   1SG.DAT   like-SUBJ.PRE.3SG   the   ice-cream
    'I think I like ice-cream.'

Notice that an infinitival competitor is not available with respect to this sentence:

(59) * *Penso   di   piacermi   il   gelato*
    think-1SG   C   like-INF-1SG.DAT   the   ice-cream
    'I think I like ice-cream.'

Thus, the status of (58) cannot be due to competition, but it can be easily explained in view of the hypothesis investigated here, because the matrix predicate implicates that the semantic content of the embedded clause is indirect, whereas the embedded clause expresses a proposition accessible through introspection. Thus, here again, a semantic clash arises between the implicatures introduced by the sentence and the semantics of the embedded clause.

7   Concluding Remarks

In this paper I have examined explored the hypothesis that subjunctive obviation in doxastic environments can be accounted for as a result of an epistemic access effect. Elaborating on Schlenker's (2005) notion of "event *de se*" I have developed an analysis of obviation and of obviation weakening facts whereby in doxastic attitudes that display obviation the propositional content expressed in the embedded clause is object of self-knowledge – that is, it is accessible through introspection – whereas in environment where the obviative interpretation is dropped the propositional content expressed in the embedded clause is otherwise accessible (for instance, through demonstration or inference). I have then explored the hypothesis that obviation is due to a clash between the semantics of doxastic predicates and that of embedded clauses. Some consequences of this analysis have then been discussed. Contrary to what has been traditionally assumed, obviation does not involve only subjunctive clauses but can also obtain in indicative clauses as long as the matrix verb implies an indirect access to the proposition and the embedded clause refers to a proposition that is accessed introspectively. Moreover, other epistemic access effects have been discussed, showing that previously unnoticed phenomena concerning epistemic predicates and embedded clauses including psych-verbs stem from the very same semantic clash causing obviation, which provides independent evidence in favor of the device proposed here to account for obviation.

References

Aikhenvald, Alexandra Y. 2004. *Evidentiality*. Oxford: Oxford University Press.
Avrutin, Sergey. 1994. Psycholinguistics investigations in the theory of reference. Ph.D. diss., MIT.
Avrutin, Sergey, Babyonyshev, Maria. 1997. Obviation in subjunctive clauses and Agr: evidence from Russian. *Natural Language and Linguistic Theory* 15: 229–267.

Belletti, Adriana, Rizzi, Luigi. 1988. Psych-Verbs and Θ-Theory. *Natural Language and Linguistic Theory* 6: 291–352.

Bergqvist, Henrik, Kittilä, Seppo. 2017. Person and knowledge: Introduction. *Open Linguistics* 3: 18–30.

Bergqvist, Henrik, Kittilä, Seppo. 2020. Epistemicity perspectives: Evidentiality, egophoricity, and engagement. In *Evidentiality, egophoricity, and engagement* ed. Henrik Bergqvist and Seppo Kittilä, 1–21. Berlin: Language Science Press.

Bouchard, Denis. 1984. *On the Content of Empty Categories*. Dordrecht: Foris.

Burge, Tyler. 1988. Individualism and Self-Knowledge. *The Journal of Philosophy* 85: 649–663.

Burge, Tyler. 1996. Our Entitlement to Self-Knowledge: I. *Proceedings of the Aristotelian Society* 96: 91–116.

Burge, Tyler. 2007. *Foundations of Mind*. Oxford: OUP.

Castaneda, Hector-Neri. 1966. He*: A Study in the Logic of Self-Consciousness. *Ratio* 8: 130–157.

Chafe, Wallace, Nichols, Johanna (eds.), 1986. *Evidentiality: The Linguistic Coding of Epistemology*, Norwood, NJ: Ablex.

Chemla, Emmanuel. 2008. An Epistemic Step for Anti-Presuppositions. *Journal of Semantics*, 25/2: 141–173.

Copley, Bridget. 2008. The Plan's the Thing: Deconstructing Futurate Meaning. *Linguistic Inquiry* 39: 261–274.

Costantini, Francesco. 2010. *Interface perspectives on clausal complementation. The case of subjunctive obviation*. Venice: Cafoscarina.

Costantini, Francesco. 2013. Evidence for the competition-based analysis of subjunctive obviation from relative and adverbial clauses in Italian. In *Romance Languages and Linguistic Theory 2011. Selected Papers from 'Going Romance' Utrecht 2011*, eds. Sergio Baauw, Frank Drijkoningen, Luisa Meroni and Manuela Pinto, 75–92. Amsterdam: John Benjamins.

Costantini, Francesco. 2016. Subject obviation as a semantic failure. A preliminary account. *Annali di Ca' Foscari. Serie occidentale* 50: 109–131.

Davis, Christopher, Potts, Christopher, Speas, Margaret. 2007. The Pragmatic Values of Evidential Sentences. In *Proceedings of SALT 17*, eds. Masayuki Gibson and Tova Friedman, 71–88. Ithaca, NY: CLC Publications.

Epstein, Samuel David. 1984. Quantifier-PRO and the LF representation of PRO$_{arb}$. *Linguistic Inquiry* 20: 499–505.

Everaert, Martin. 1986. Long Reflexivization and Obviation in the Romance Languages. In *Formal Parameters of Generative Grammar*, eds. Peter Coopmans, Ivonne Bordelois, Bill Dotson Smith, 51–71. Dordrecht: Foris.

Faller, Martina. 2011. A possible worlds semantics for Cuzco Quechua evidentials, in *Proceedings of SALT 20*, eds. David Lutz and Nan Li, 660–683. Ithaca, NY: LSA and CLC Publications. Also in *Evidentials and Modal*, eds. Chungmin Lee, Jinho Park, 41–68. Leiden/Boston: Brill, 2021.

Farkas, Donka. 1988. On obligatory control. *Linguistics and Philosophy* 11: 27–58.
Farkas, Donka. 1992. On Obviation. In *Lexical Matters*, eds. Ivan A. Sag, Anna Szabolcsi, 85–109. Stanford University: CSLI.
von Fintel, Kay, Gillies, Anthony S. 2010. Must ... stay ... strong! *Natural Language Semantics* 18: 351–383.
Garrett, Edward J. 2001. Evidentiality and Assertion in Tibetan. Ph.D. diss. UCLA.
Gazdar, Gerald. 1979. *Pragmatics: Implicature, Presupposition and Logical Form*. New York: Academic Press.
Giannakidou, Aanastasia, Mari, Alda. 2016. Epistemic Future and Epistemic MUST: Nonveridicality, Evidence, and Partial Knowledge. In *Mood, Aspect, Modality Revisited. New answers to old questions*, eds. Johanna Blaszack, Joanna et al., 75–124. Chicago: University of Chicago Press.
Goncharov, Julia. 2020. Decisive modality and intentionality effect. Ms. University of Göttingen.
Goodhue, Daniel. 2017. Must φ is felicitous only if φ is not known. *Semantics and Pragmatics*, 10, 14. DOI: https://doi.org/10.3765/sp.10.14.
Hargreaves, David. 2005. Agency and intentional action in Kathmandu Newar. *Himalayan Linguistics* 5: 1–48.
Higginbotham, James. 2003. Remembering, Imagining, and the First Person. In *Epistemology of Language*, ed. Alex Barber, 496–533. Oxford: Oxford University Press.
Higginbotham, James. 2009. Evidentials: Some preliminary distinctions. In *Compositionality, Context and Semantic Values*, eds. Robert J. Stainton and Christopher Viger, 221–235. London: Springer.
Hornstein, Norbert, San Martin, Itziar. 2001. Obviation as anti-control. *Anuario Del Seminario De Filología Vasca "Julio De Urquijo"* 35: 367–384.
Izvorski, Roumyana. 1997. The Present Perfect as an Epistemic Modal. In *Proceedings of SALT 7*, ed. Aaron Lawson, 222–239. Ithaca, NY: Cornell University.
Karttunen, Lauri. 1972. Possible and Must. *Syntax and Semantics*, 1: 1–20.
Kaufmann, Magdalena. 2019. Who controls who (or what). In *Proceedings of SALT 29*, eds. Katherine Blake, Forrest Davis, Kaelyn Lamp, and Joseph Rhyne, 636–664. Ithaca, NY: LSA and CLC Publications.
Kaufmann, Magdalena. 2020. A semantic-pragmatic account of generalized subject obviation. Colloquium at Georg-August-University, Göttingen, May 2020.
Kempchinsky, Paula. 1987. The subjunctive disjoint reference effect. In *Studies in Romance Linguistics*, eds. Carol Neidle, Rafael Nuñez Cedeño, 123–140. Dordrecht: Foris.
Kempchinsky, Paula. 1998. Mood Phrase, Case Checking and Obviation. In *Romance Linguistics: Theoretical Perspectives*, eds. Armin Schwegler, Bernard Tranel, Myriam Uribe-Etxebarria, 143–154. Amsterdam/Philadelphia: John Benjamins.
Kempchinsky, Paula. 2009. What can the subjunctive disjoint reference effect tell us about the subjunctive? *Lingua* 119: 1788–1810.

Kittilä, Seppo. 2019. General knowledge as an evidential category. *Linguistics* 57: 1271–1304.

Levinson, Stephen. 1983. *Pragmatics*. Cambridge: Cambridge University Press.

Manzini, Maria Rita. 2000. Sentential complementation. The subjunctive. In *Lexical Specification and Insertion*, eds. Peter Coopmans, Martin Everaert, Jane Grimshaw, 241–267. Amsterdam/Philadelphia: John Benjamins.

Mari, Alda. 2016. Assertability conditions on epistemic (and fictional) attitudes and mood variation. In *Proceedings of SALT 26*, eds. Mary Moroney, Carol-Rose Little, Jacob Collard, and Dan Burgdorf, 61–81. Ithaca, NY: LSA and CLC Publications.

Mari, Alda, Portner, Paul. 2021. Mood variation with belief predicates: Modal comparison and raisability of questions. *Glossa* 40/1: 132.

Picallo, Carme. 1985. Opaque domains. Ph.D. diss., CUNY.

Progovac, Ljiljana. 1994. *Negative and Positive Polarity: a Binding Approach*. Cambridge: Cambridge University Press.

Progovac, Ljiljana. 1993. Subjunctive: the (mis)behavior of anaphora and negative polarity. *The Linguistic Review* 10: 37–59.

Pryor, James. 1999. Immunity to error through misidentification. *Philosophical Topics* 26: 271–307.

Raposo, Eduardo. 1985. Some asymmetries in the Binding Theory in Romance. *The Linguistic Review* 5: 75–110.

Recanati, François. 2007. *Perspectival Thought*. Oxford: Oxford University Press.

Rizzi, Luigi. 1991. On the anaphor-agreement effect. In *Comparative Syntax and Language Acquisition*, Luigi Rizzi, 158–173. London/New York: Routledge.

Ruwet, Nicolas. 1984. Je veux partir / *Je veux que je parte: on the distribution of finite complements and infinitival complements in French. *Cahiers de Grammaire* 7: 75–138.

Schlenker, Philippe. 2005. The Lazy Frenchman's approach to the subjunctive (speculations on reference to worlds, presuppositions, and semantic defaults in the analysis of mood). In *Romance Languages and Linguistic Theory 2003*, eds. Twan Geerts, Ivo van Ginneken, Haike Jacobs, 269–309. Amsterdam/Philadelphia: John Benjamins.

Shoemaker, Sydney. 1968. Self-Reference and Self-Awareness. *Journal of Philosophy* 65: 555–67.

Simons, Mandy. 2007. Observations on embedding verbs, evidentiality, and presupposition. *Lingua* 117: 1034–1056.

Speas, Margaret, Kalsang, Jay Garfield, Jill de Villiers. 2013. Direct evidentials, case, tense and aspect in Tibetan: evidence for a general theory of the semantics of evidential. *Natural Language & Linguist Theory* 31: 517–561.

Squartini, Mario. 2001. The internal structure of evidentiality in Romance. *Studies in Language* 25: 297–334.

Squartini, Mario. 2008. Lexical vs. grammatical evidentiality in French and Italian. *Linguistics* 46: 917–947.

Squartini, Mario. 2018. Extragrammatical expression of information source. In *The Oxford Handbook of Evidentiality*, ed. Alexandra Y. Aikhenvald, 273–285. Oxford: Oxford University Press.

Suñer, Margarita. 1986. On the referential properties of embedded finite clause subjects. In *Generative Studies in Spanish Syntax*, eds. Ivonne Bordelois, Helas Contreras, Karen Zagona, 183–196. Dordrecht: Foris.

Szabolcsi, Anna. 2010. Infinitive vs. subjunctives. What do we learn from obviation and from exemptions from obviation? Ms. NYU. https://philarchive.org/rec/SZAIVS.

Szabolcsi, Anna. 2021. Obviation in Hungarian: what is its scope, and is it due to competition? *Glossa: a journal of general linguistics* 6. DOI: https://doi.org/10.5334/gjgl.1421.

Tsoulas, George. 1996. The nature of the subjunctive and the formal grammar of obviation. In *Grammatical Theory and Romance Languages*, ed. Karen Zagona, 293–306. Amsterdam/Philadelphia: John Benjamins.

Willett, Thomas. 1988. A Cross-Linguistic Survey of the Grammaticization of Evidentiality. *Studies in Language* 12: 51–97.

Two Semantic Paths to Unintentional Causation

Ömer Demirok
Boğaziçi University, Turkey
omerfaruk.demirok@boun.edu.tr

Abstract

Some languages have special constructions which appear to encode unintentional causation. In previous research, two distinct ways of deriving this reading have been proposed: one that involves a circumstantial necessity modal and one that involves introducing a possessor onto a change of state event. While in the former unintentional causation boils down to an event being forced by circumstances, in the latter it is derived as an implicature in the absence of a canonical agent relation in syntax. In this paper, I investigate two morphosyntactically distinct constructions in Laz (South Caucasian) which both allow the unintentional causation reading. I show that these two constructions instantiate the proposed distinct semantic paths to unintentional causation, providing empirical evidence that the modal and the non-modal paths can co-exist in a grammar. The investigation also reveals that what enables the modal path in Laz is a circumstantial possibility modal, which exhibits force variability in the absence of its dual.

Keywords

unintentional causation – circumstantial modals – force variable modals – oblique causers

1   Introduction

Many natural languages have morphosyntactically distinguished "un-agentive" constructions in which an agent's relation to an event is understood as *not* prototypical. For example, given that it is prototypical of agents to intend their actions, we may expect an un-agentive construction to license an inference as in (1).

(1)   where A = agent
      A did not intend to do x, but accidentally did x

In (2), we have two examples of such morphosyntactically distinguished un-agentive constructions from St'át'imcets and German, respectively. The English translations of these sentences suggest that speakers of St'át'imcets and German associate these sentences with an inference of the kind in (1). Notably, neither of the sentences seems to have an element that directly contributes what the adverb *accidentally* contributes to the English sentences. Yet, the inferences (if not truth conditions) that derive from these constructions seem to warrant English translations that feature the adverb *accidentally*.

(2) a. ka-sek'w-s-as-a ta=nk'wanusten'=a ta=tweww'et=a
OOC-break-CAUS-3ERG-OOC DET=window=EXIS DET=boy=EXIS
'The boy broke the window *accidentally*.' (*St'át'imcets*, Davis et al. (2009): p. 212)
b. mir ist der Teller heruntergefallen
I.DAT be.PRS.3SG the.NOM plate fall.down.PARTC
'I *accidentally* dropped the plate.' (*German*, Kittilä (2005): p. 414)

As will be discussed in the following section, the un-agentive constructions in St'át'imcets and German have been given different analyses: a modal analysis and a non-modal analysis respectively. Given the parallelism in the type of inference that derives from these constructions, it is an intriguing question whether the two semantic paths proposed to derive this inference of unintentional causation can co-exist in the same grammar.[1] In this paper, I attempt to answer this question empirically by investigating Laz, an endangered South Caucasian language spoken in Turkey. I will show that Laz exhibits two varieties of un-agentive constructions, illustrated in (3), which contrast with the canonical agentive sentence in (4).[2] I will show that there are important asymmetries between the two un-agentive constructions and argue that the two constructions instantiate the non-modal and modal paths to unintentional causation, respectively.

---

1 I assume that two 'semantic paths' are distinct if we derive distinct truth conditions from them. In this paper, I use the expression 'semantic path' in order to highlight the fact that the difference between two analyses is not only syntactic.
2 Laz examples use the following glossing abbreviations: APPL = applicative, CAUS = causative, COMP = complementizer, COND = conditional, DAT = dative, ERG = ergative, GEN = genitive, IMP = imperative, IMPF = imperfective, PL = plural, POS = possessive, PRS = present, PV = preverb, PST = past tense, NEG = negation, NOM = nominative, SG = singular.

(3) a. Bere-s   t'abaği   [u]-   t'rox   -u
       child-DAT   plate.NOM   APPL.3   break_intrns   -PST
       'The child *accidentally* broke the plate.'

   b. Bere-s   t'abaği   [a]-   t'ax   -u
       child-DAT   plate.NOM   MODAL   break_trans   -PST
       'The child *accidentally* broke the plate.'

(4) Bere-k   t'abaği   t'ax   -u
    child-ERG   plate.NOM   break_trans -PST
    'The child broke the plate.'

This paper is structured as follows. In section 2, I provide some typological and theoretical background on what I referred to as un-agentive constructions and discuss the two proposals to derive unintentional causation inferences. In section 3, I introduce the two un-agentive constructions in Laz and lay out the syntactic asymmetries between them. In section 4, I discuss the interpretational asymmetries between the two constructions. Section 5 ends the paper with questions for future research.

2 Background on Un-agentive Constructions

2.1 *Background in Typological Research*

What I have referred to as un-agentive constructions have primarily featured in typological work under the name *Involuntary Agent Construction* (Haspelmath, 1993; Kittilä, 2005; Fauconnier, 2011, a.o.).[3] As Kittilä (2005) argues, constructions typologically classified as Involuntary Agent Construction typically have some special marking on the understood agent, or on the verb, or both.

In Lezgian, for example, a canonical agent is ergative, as shown in (5a), while the agent NP gets an oblique case (*adelative*) in the Involuntary Agent Construction, as shown in (5b). On the surface, there is no morphological change in the verb.[4]

---

3 Kittilä (2005) attributes the use of this term to Haspelmath (1993).
4 Though Haspelmath (1993) argues that the surface no-alternation on the verb is possible only when the verb is labile (i.e. participates in the causative alternation without any morphological marking in either directions). He notes that transitive roots that are not labile cannot be used in the Involuntary Agent Construction in the absence of any additional morphosyntactic manipulation.

(5) a. Zamara.di   get'e   xa-na
       Zamira.ERG   pot   break-AOR
       'Zamira broke the pot.'

   b. Zamara.di-*waj* get'e   xa-na
      Zamira-ADEL   pot   break-AOR
      'Zamira broke the pot *accidentally*.' (*Lezgian*, Haspelmath (1993): p. 292)

In Guugu Yimidhirr, on the other hand, we see additional anti-causative marking (i.e. intransitivizing morphology) on the verb while the understood agent again bears some oblique case (*adessive*).

(6) a. Ngayu   galga   nhanu   dumbi
       1SG.NOM   spear   2SG.GEN   break.PST
       'I broke your spear'

   b. Ngadhun-*gal* galga   nhanu   dumbi-:*dhi*
      1SG-ADESS   spear   2SG.GEN   break.PST-ANTIC
      'I *accidentally* broke your spear.' (*Guugu Yimidhirr*, Haviland (1979): pp. 125, 149)

Kittilä (2005) argues that such morphosyntactic manipulations, exemplified by Lezgian and Guugu Yimidhirr above, primarily signal "… the involuntary participation of agents in events, i.e. they have not intended nor wanted to be an agent in the event profiled." (p. 382). This is what I will call the *unintentional causation* inference, the primary 'function' associated with the Involuntary Agent Construction. However, Kittilä argues that cross-linguistically Involuntary Agent Constructions often exhibit *polysemy*.[5] For example, in Japanese, the Involuntary Agent Construction, whose primary function is exemplified in (7a), can also be used to describe a situation where an agent "finally or unexpectedly *managestodosomething*", as shown in (7b).

---

5   I adopt the term *polysemy* from Kittilä. I should clarify at this point that I use the term descriptively to refer to the availability of multiple readings and certainly do not intend to allude to an analysis by it. As a reviewer rightly points out, the use of the term 'polysemy' in its technical sense does not sound appropriate when used in the context of the modal analysis to be discussed in the next subsection.

(7) a. kodomo ga   isu   o   kowashite shimatta
       child   NOM   chair ACC break:*te* come(AUX).PST
       'The child accidentally broke the chair.'

   b. kodomo ga   otona o   mochiagete shimatta
       child   NOM adult ACC lift.up:*te* come(AUX).PST
       'The child managed to lift the adult up (unexpectedly).' (*Japanese*, Kittilä (2005): p. 411)

The label Involuntary Agent Construction may seem odd for a sentence like (7b) in that the agent does try and intend to do what they manage to do (albeit unexpectedly). Nevertheless, Kittilä argues that in (7b) the agent has a "lower degree of control", alluding to the fact that the agent's action does not in any way guarantee the observed consequence. Since the strength of a child normally wouldn't suffice to lift an adult up, then, perhaps, the agent is not fully 'in control' in the sense that there is some other factor involved – perhaps, luck. From this perspective, this additional interpretation could belong in the class of constructions that morphosyntactically indicate that an agent's relation to an event is not prototypical. As will be discussed in the next section, theoretical research tries to accommodate this polysemy issue in different ways.

2.2 Background in Theoretical Research

Broadly, there are two notable theoretical approaches to un-agentive constructions: a modal approach and a non-modal approach. I discuss these in the following subsections, starting with the non-modal approach.

2.2.1 A Non-modal Approach

A non-modal account of un-agentive constructions was developed in Schäfer (2008, 2009), building on Cuervo (2003) in particular. In what follows, I discuss the account Schäfer (2008, 2009) offers for Involuntary Agent Construction, which he calls Oblique Causer Construction. There are two key aspects of this proposal. First, the VP is intransitive and denotes a change of state event. Second, what introduces the oblique causer is not a voice head (or a special kind of cause head) but an applicative head. Following Cuervo (2003), Schäfer (2008, 2009) argues that what relates the NP to the VP is an applicative head with a reduced semantics of 'possession', as diagrammed in (8). Essentially, this structure contrasts with a regular causative/transitive structure where the agent is introduced by voice (Kratzer, 1996), as shown in (9).

(8)

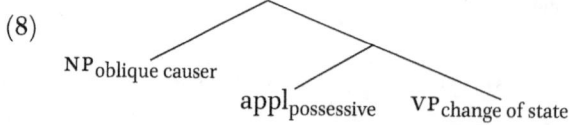

(9)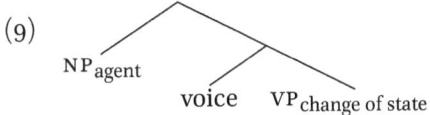
NP$_{agent}$ voice   VP$_{change\ of\ state}$

The most intriguing part of this proposal is that appl$_{possessive}$ does not introduce the NP in its specifier as a [-intentional] causer. The relation that appl$_{possessive}$ brings in is more abstract (and vague), which Schäfer (2008) argues allows the NP to be construed as the *source* of the change of state event. But how does appl$_{possessive}$ end up giving rise to the unintentional causation interpretation? The idea here seems to be that the structures in (8) and (9) compete. Schäfer (2008) writes that the unintentional causation interpretation is "... is just a pragmatic implication of the fact that the construction cannot actively assert intentionality" (p. 114).[6]

As mentioned above, a key feature of this proposal is that the VP is intransitive and denotes a change of state event. This points to a well-established cross-linguistic observation regarding un-agentive constructions that give rise to the unintentional causation interpretation. As Schäfer (2008) and Fauconnier (2011) both argue at length, oblique NPs construed as unintentional causers can only combine with anticausative verbs.[7] This appears to be a cross-linguistic generalization.[8] For example, in Tsez we see that the oblique NP interpreted as an oblique causer in (10c) goes with the anticausative verb in (10a) rather than the causative verb in (10b). Similarly, we expect to see intransitivizing morphology appear on a non-labile causative verb when an oblique causer is added to it, as was shown to be the case for Guugu Yimidhirr in (6).

(10) a. č'ikay   y-exu-s
        glass.ABS   II-break-PAST.WIT
        'The glass broke.'

---

6   Admittedly, the wording in this quote may make it sound like whatever introduces an agent NP should have the property of 'actively asserting intentionality', which also cannot be true. I believe that it should suffice for an implicature to be derived that the hearer reasons as follows: 'if this NP were an intentional causer, it would have been introduced as an agent because agents are more prototypically intentional causers. Since it has not been introduced as an agent, it may be an unintentional causer.'

7   I use the term anticausative to refer to any verbal predicate that has a change of state semantics but does not license an external argument explicitly (as in transitives) or implicitly (as in passives). I also follow Schäfer (2009) in assuming that anticausative change of state events are inherently causative. Their only difference from transitive change of state verbs is that they lack an external argument as well as the head that introduces it (Kratzer, 1996).

8   See also Haspelmath (1993) for Lezgian.

b. už-ā   č' ikay   y-exu-r-si
   boy-ERG   glass.ABS   II-break-CAUS-PAST.WIT
   'The boy broke the glass.'

c. uži-q   č' ikay   y-exu-s
   boy-POSS   glass.ABS   II-break-PAST.WIT
   'The boy accidentally broke the glass.' (*Tsez*, Schäfer (2008): p. 112)

Finally, Schäfer (2009) argues that this account can accommodate various readings of the Oblique Causer Construction (recall the *polysemy* issue briefly discussed in the previous section). The idea is that the appl$_{possessive}$ which relates the oblique NP to the event has a meaning that is vague enough to allow various readings for the oblique NP. Recall that in run-of-the-mill possessive constructions, the relationship between the possessor and the possessee is largely contextually determined, as illustrated in (11).

(11) Mary's movie:
   (i) the movie that Mary has been non-stop talking about,
   (ii) the movie that Mary appeared in, etc.

The polysemy that Involuntary Agent/Oblique Causer Construction exhibits is characterized in Ganenkov et al. (2008) for Agul as illustrated in (12).

(12) ruš.a-f-as   rak̄   daqu-ne.
     girl.AD.ELAT   door.ABS   open-PERF (*Agul*, Schäfer (2008): p. 107)

   READING-I: The girl accidentally opened the door (because she pushed it with her elbow while playing with her toys on the floor).

   READING-II: (The father told the girl to hold the door so that the wind could not open it, but her efforts were not enough.) The girl accidentally opened the door/let the door open.

   READING-III: (All the children tried but no one could open the tightly closed door, however it so happened that) The girl managed to open the door.

In READING-I, the oblique causer is doing something without noticing, unintentionally causing a change of state. In READING-II, what causes the change of state is not the oblique causer but some other force. However, the oblique causer has a role of unintentional facilitation by failing to prevent that force from causing the change of state. In READING-III, on the other hand, the change of state *is* intended by the oblique causer but it seems unusual that the change of state that has occurred is due to the oblique causer alone. Then, READING-III alludes to some other factor/effector being behind the observed change of state, designating the relation of the oblique causer to the event as not prototypical. As Schäfer (2008) rightly points out the oblique causer could not have a specification such as [-intentional] given that READING-III does not even feature a [-intentional] causer (also see the example in (7b) for comparable data in Japanese). However, the vague semantics of possession that Schäfer (2008) argues for may indeed accommodate all of these situations where the relation of the agent to the event is not prototypical.

2.2.2 A Modal Approach

Davis et al. (2009) propose a modal analysis for the *out-of-control* circumfix ka- ... -a in St'át'imcets, cited, for example, in Fauconnier (2011) as an example of Involuntary Agent Construction. Notably, sentences that feature the *out-of-control* circumfix also exhibit the two readings described under the term 'polysemy' in Kittilä (2005). As shown in the examples in (13a) and (13b), both unintentional causation and *manage-to* readings are available to the *out-of-control* marking in St'át'imcets.

(13) a. *ka*-sek'w-s-as-*a*   ta=nk'wanusten'=a ta=tweww'et=a
    OOC-break-CAUS-3ERG-OOC   DET=window=EXIS DET=boy=EXIS
    'The boy broke the window *accidentally*'

  b. *ka*-gwél-s=kan-*a*
    OOC-burn-CAUS-1SG.SUBJ-OOC
    'I managed to get it lit.' (*St'át'imcets*, Davis et al. (2009): pp. 211, 212)

What Davis et al. (2009) propose for the out-of-control marking is substantially different from Schäfer's appl$_{possessive}$. They argue that the out-of-control marker expones a *circumstantial modal*, which happens to exhibit force ambiguity in the language, allowing both existential (possibility) and universal (necessity) construals. In particular, the unintentional causation reading arises when the modal force is universal while the *manage-to* interpretation arises when the modal force is existential.[9] Accordingly, the St'át'imcets sentences above have the paraphrases indicated in (14). An event is circumstantially possible if circumstances of that event (and its participants) *allow* that event to unfold whereas an event is circumstantially necessary if circumstances of that event (and its participants) *force* that event to unfold.

(14) a. It was *circumstantially necessary* for the boy to break the window.
 ≈ (13a)
 b. It was *circumstantially possible* for me to get it lit. ≈ (13b)

Hence, the availability of the two readings which Kittilä (2005) categorizes as polysemy is addressed in a deterministic manner under the modal approach, predicting two sets of meanings that fall under necessity and possibility construals. Since all modals in St'át'imcets are systematically force ambiguous (Rullmann et al., 2008), it is not surprising for the circumstantial modal to exhibit both universal and existential readings. Accordingly, under this approach, what Kittilä (2005) describes as polysemy is predicted to be parasitic on the presence of force ambiguity in the circumstantial modal (however force ambiguity may be analyzed in the end). For instance, the modal approach to unintentional causation was also adopted in Rivero et al. (2010) for Involuntary State Construction in Polish, which reportedly only has readings consistent with the modal being a circumstantial necessity modal.

2.2.3 Interim Discussion

In this section, we have seen modal and non-modal analyses of unintentional causation inferences: one that involves a circumstantial necessity modal and the other that posits a head that establishes a non-canonical thematic relation between change of state events and individuals (in particular, the relation of possession). There are a number of questions about both of these proposals. For example, in the non-modal analysis, it is not clear what blocks a possession relation to be established with activities (i.e. what restricts the relevant relation to change of state events). Likewise, in the modal analysis, it is not obvious that circumstantial necessity modals are cross-linguistically felicitous in unintentional causation contexts. Although both analyses may be leaving some

---

9 It may not be immediately clear how unintentional causation derives from circumstantial necessity. Here, the idea is that an unintentional action is in essence an accidental event forced to unfold as a necessary consequence of its circumstances.

questions unresolved, they do make different empirical predictions, which is what the rest of this paper will be focusing on.

Another intriguing question that I have to set aside in this paper is whether the two proposed semantic paths could be shown to share a common core. While circumstantial necessity and causality are standardly taken to be distinct notions, there is also a highly promising line of work that uses causality to model some modal notions (Nadathur, 2019, 2020; Copley, 2021). In this paper, I abstract away from this intriguing possibility, which merits an independent investigation beyond the scope of this study. Instead, I take it for granted that natural languages do allow the two semantic paths to unintentional causation and demonstrate that the two paths can co-exist in the grammar of a single language, as instantiated by the two un-agentive constructions in Laz.

In the following section, I discuss the syntactic contrasts between the two un-agentive constructions in Laz. In section 4, I turn to the interpretational asymmetries between them.

3   Syntactic Contrasts

Two distinct constructions can express unintentional causation in Laz, as shown in (15).[10] They are distinguished by the pre-root vowel they choose. In a way that foreshadows the analyses I will adopt for them, I will gloss the pre-root vowel *i-* as APPL and the pre-root vowel *a-* as MODAL. And accordingly, I will refer to the constructions as Oblique Causer Construction and Circumstantial Modal Construction, respectively.[11]

(15) a. t'abaği   m-   [i]-   t'rox   -u
       plate.NOM   1-   APPL   break$_{intrns}$ -PST
       'I *accidentally* broke the plate.' Oblique Causer Construction (OCC)

---

10 The Laz data reported here has been elicited through fieldwork with the speakers of the Pazar (Atina) dialect of Laz (Öztürk and Pöchtrager, 2011). I owe my thanks to my primary consultant İsmail Bucaklişi and two other Pazar Laz speakers for their generous help and patience.

11 In both constructions, the understood causer is an oblique NP (i.e. DAT in Laz), as shown in (18). In order not to invent yet another name for the Oblique Causer Construction, I follow Schäfer (2008, 2009) and keep using this term even though it is not particularly informative in the context of Laz.

b. t'abaği   m-   boxed{a}-   t'ax   -u
plate.NOM   1-   MODAL   break$_{trans}$ -PST
'I *accidentally* broke the plate.' Circumstantial Modal Construction (CMC)

As indicated in the glosses, the roots that *t'ax* 'break' and *t'rox* 'break' differ in transitivity. While *t'ax* is a transitive verb, *t'rox* is an intransitive verb, as shown in the examples in (16) and (17).

(16) a. Bere-k   t'abaği   t'ax   -u
child-ERG   plate.NOM   break$_{trans}$ -PST
'The child broke the plate.' transitive/causative

b. *Bere-k   t'abaği   t'rox   -u
child-ERG   plate.NOM   break$_{intrns}$ -PST
Intended: 'The child broke the plate.'

(17) a. T'abaği   t'rox   -u
plate.NOM   break$_{intrns}$ -PST
'The plate broke.' intransitive/anticausative

b. *T'abaği   t'ax   -u
plate.NOM   break$_{trans}$ -PST
Intended: 'The plate broke.'

An orthogonal point that needs to be mentioned here to avoid confusion later is that the pre-root vowel *i-* changes to *u-* if the oblique NP (*dative*) is third person, as shown in (18). The pre-root vowel *a-*, however, is invariant across different agreement paradigms.

(18) a. Bere-s   t'abaği   boxed{u}-   t'rox   -u
child-DAT   plate.NOM   APPL.3   break$_{intrns}$ -PST
'The child *accidentally* broke the plate.' OCC

b. Bere-s   t'abaği   boxed{a}-   t'ax   -u
child-DAT   plate.NOM   MODAL   break$_{trans}$ -PST
'The child *accidentally* broke the plate.' CMC

In two subsections that follow, I discuss the internal structures of these constructions, in particular what kinds of syntactic objects APPL and MODAL combine with. Throughout the discussion in this section, we will limit the discussion to the structural properties of OCC and CMC and turn to the question of what range of meanings OCC and CMC can express in Section 4.

3.1   The Syntactic Anatomy of the Oblique Causer Construction in Laz

The Oblique Causer Construction in Laz is fully parallel to its counterparts reported to exist in other languages. The oblique NP systematically combines with an intransitive change of state VP. Hence, the decomposition that Schäfer (2008) argues for the Oblique Causer Construction seems suitable for its Laz counterpart.

(19) a. t'abaği   t'rox   -u
        plate.NOM   break$_{intrns}$ -PST
        'The plate broke.' simple anticausative

    b. Ma   tabaği   m-   i-   t'rox   -u
       I.DAT   plate.NOM   1-   APPL- break$_{intrns}$ -PST
       'I *accidentally* broke the plate.' OCC

Accordingly, I argue that the example in (19b) has the structure in (20), building on the anticausative VP that the sentence in (19a) embeds.

(20)
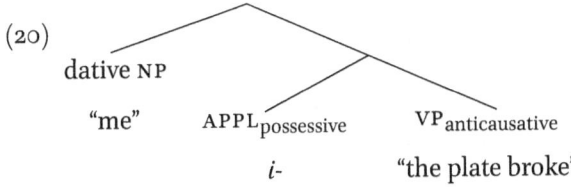
dative NP
"me"   APPL$_{possessive}$ VP$_{anticausative}$
         i-   "the plate broke"

Given this composition and in particular the stipulation that the APPL$_{possessive}$ combines with an intransitive change of state VP, overt causativizers are predicted to be ruled out in this construction. This is indeed the case, as shown below.

Unaccusative predicates regularly require the causative suffix *-in* in the causative alternation, as shown in the sentence pair in (21). However, OCC does not tolerate the *-in* suffix, as shown by the contrast in (22).

(21) a. K'oğoni   do-   ğur   -u
        mosquito.NOM   PV-   die   -PST
        'The mosquito died.' unaccusative

b. Bere-k   k'oğoni   do- ğur -in   -u
   child-ERG   mosquito.NOM   PV- die -CAUS -PST
   'The child killed the mosquito.' derived causative

(22) a. Ma   k'oğoni   do- m- i-   ğur -u
        I.DAT mosquito.NOM   PV- 1- APPL- die -PST
        'I accidentally killed the mosquito.' OCC

   b. *Ma   k'oğoni   do- m- i-   ğur -in   -u
        I.DAT mosquito.NOM   PV- 1- APPL- die -CAUS -PST

There is also evidence that the oblique NP that APPL$_{possessive}$ relates to the VP is **not** an external argument which would normally be introduced by voice. Instruments and natural forces can be external arguments in Laz, as shown the data in (23).[12]

(23) a. Zelzele-k   tabaği   t'ax   -u
        earthquake-ERG plate.NOM   break$_{trans}$ -PST
        'The earthquake broke the plate.' external argument is force

   b. Burç'uli-k tabaği   t'ax   -u
        ax-ERG plate.NOM   break$_{trans}$ -PST
        'The ax broke the plate.' external argument is instrument

However, the oblique NP cannot be an instrument or force, showing that the oblique NP in the Oblique Causer Construction does not have an external argument status on a par with NPs introduced by voice.[13]

(24) a. #Zelzele-s   tabaği   u-   t'rox   -u
        earthquake-DAT   plate.NOM   3.APPL- break$_{intrns}$ -PST
        Intended: 'The earthquake broke the plate.' oblique NP cannot be force

---

12   Laz differentiates external vs. internal arguments through case marking. All NPs introduced in the specifier of voiceP (including subjects of unergatives) receive ERG case in Laz. See also fn.15.
13   Schäfer (2009) shows that OCC in German also comes with a [+human] restriction. He argues that this property of OCC follows from independent restrictions on applied arguments. See also McIntyre (2006) for relevant discussion.

b. #Burç'uli-s tabaği   u-   t'rox   -u
   ax-DAT   plate.NOM 3.APPL- break_intrns -PST
   Intended: 'The ax broke the plate.' oblique NP cannot be instrument

Finally, the APPL_possessive cannot combine with just any intransitive VP. The VP needs to denote a change of state event.[14] Accordingly, unergative verbs are systematically out in the Oblique Causer Construction.[15]

(25) a. Badi-k   barbal -u
        old.man-ERG   speak -PST
        'The old man spoke/nagged.'

    b. *Badi-s   u-   barbal -u
        old.man-DAT   3.APPL- speak -PST
        Intended: 'The old man accidentally spoke.'

Another noteworthy data point is that the morphosyntax of OCC is also employed to introduce possessors to theme NPs in Laz (Pylkkänen, 2002). The example in (26a) illustrates the canonical possessive construction where the possessor appears in genitive while the example in (26b) features a DAT applied argument that can be construed as a possessor to the theme NP, which is indexed on the verb by the applicative prefix u-.

(26) a. Bere-şi   layç'i   ğur -u
        child-GEN   dog.NOM   die -PST
        'The child's dog died.'

    b. Bere-s   layç'i   u-   ğur -u
        child-DAT   dog.NOM   APPL.3-   die -PST
        'The child's dog died.'

This means that the morphosyntax of OCC is almost always ambiguous between a construal where the DAT argument is an unintentional causer and construal

---

14 As far as I can tell, this needs to remain as a stipulation.
15 The unergative vs. unaccusative distinction correlates with ERG vs. NOM case marking on the sole argument, for Laz is one of the few languages with an active-ergative case alignment (Öztürk and Pöchtrager, 2011).

where the DAT argument is the possessor of the theme NP, as shown by the sentence in (27).

(27) Ma   tabaği   m-   i-   t'rox   -u
     I.DAT   plate.NOM   1-   APPL-   break$_{intrns}$ -PST
     'I *accidentally* broke the plate.'
     'My plate broke.'

One way to disambiguate the OCC morphosyntax is to have an overt genitive possessor on the theme NP, as in (28). This string only accepts the construal where the DAT argument is an unintentional causer.

(28) Badi-s   biç'i-şi   oşk'uri   u-   kts -u
     old.man-DAT   boy-GEN   apple.NOM   APPL.3-   rot -PST
     'The old man *accidentally* let the boy's apple rot.'

3.2 The Syntactic Anatomy of the Circumstantial Modal Construction in Laz

The basic property of Circumstantial Modal Construction in Laz is that the DAT argument *can* combine with transitive verbs, unlike in OCC. Considering the sentence pair in (29), we see two surface alternations in building the Circumstantial Modal Construction: The pre-root vowel *a-* is prefixed to the verbal root and the ERG NP is replaced by a DAT NP.

(29) a. Arte-*k*   ist'ik'anepe   t'ax   -u
        Arte-ERG   glasses.NOM   break   PST
        'Arte broke the glasses.' basic transitive

     b. Arte-*s*   ist'ik'anepe   [a]-   t'ax   -u
        Arte-DAT   glasses.NOM   MODAL- break   -PST
        'Arte *accidentally* broke the glasses.' CMC

Building on earlier work (Öztürk, 2013; Demirok, 2013, 2018), I argue that the circumstantial modal head exponed by the pre-root vowel *a-* combines with an unsaturated voiceP.[16] The composition is quite similar to the way the passive

---

[16] In Öztürk (2013), voiceP is not unsaturated as there is a null element in its specifier that gets bound by the oblique NP. I translate that composition to a simpler syntax where binding is done in the meaning composition.

head combines with an unsaturated voiceP in Bruening (2013). What's different here is that the modal head saturates the voiceP in its complement with the NP merged in its specifier, as diagrammed in (30). A key aspect of this proposed composition is that the oblique NP is an external argument since it ends up saturating the unsaturated voiceP in the semantic composition even though it is syntactically introduced in the specifier of a modal head that selects an unsaturated voiceP.[17]

(30)

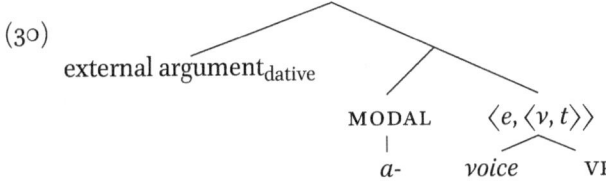

external argument_dative

MODAL ⟨e, ⟨v, t⟩⟩
|
a- voice VP

The composition above is motivated by the fact that the MODAL head cannot combine with anticausative verbs, as shown in (31) and (32).

(31) a. Ditsxiri   do-   k'ort   -u
       blood.NOM   PV-   clot_intrns -PST
       'The blood clotted.' anticausative

   b. *Ma   ditsxiri   do-   m-   a-   k'ort   -u
      I.DAT blood.NOM PV- 1-   MODAL- clot_intrns -PST
      Intended: 'I *accidentally* let the blood clot.'

(32) a. K'oğoni   do-   ğur   -u
       mosquito.NOM   PV-   die   -PST
       'The mosquito died.' anticausative base

   b. *Ma   k'oğoni   do-   m-   a-   ğur   -u
      I.DAT mosquito.NOM   PV- 1-   APPL-   die   -PST
      Intended: 'I *accidentally* killed the mosquito.'

---

17 It is noteworthy that the MODAL head here assigns DAT to the NP in its specifier. From this perspective, the MODAL head is just like the APPL head in OCC assigning DAT to the NP in its specifier. In order not to create confusion in glosses, I gloss a- as MODAL, not as APPL. See also Rivero et al. (2010) where the Polish Circumstantial Modal is assumed to be an APPL head and Demirok (2018) where the modal semantics is located in an APPL head.

Since the MODAL head cannot combine with an anticausative vP, overt causativizers are required. If we assume that causativizers expone Kratzer's voice (Kratzer, 2005; Deal, 2009), this constitutes evidence for the claim that the MODAL head selects for a voiceP.

(33) a. Bere-k   k'oğoni   do-   ğur   -in   -u
        child-ERG mosquito.NOM PV-   die   -CAUS -PST
        'The child killed the mosquito.' derived causative

   b. Ma   k'oğoni   do- m-   a-   ğur   -in   -u
      I.DAT mosquito.NOM PV- 1-   MODAL- die   -CAUS -PST
      'I accidentally killed the mosquito.' CMC

Moreover, since the MODAL head saturates this voiceP with the oblique NP in its specifier, we predict that the oblique NP will accept the full range of roles for external arguments, including instruments. This is borne out as shown in (34). Recall that this is not possible in OCC where the oblique NP cannot be an instrument, as shown by the example repeated in (35).

(34) Burç'uli-s tabaği   a-   t'ax   -u
     ax-DAT   plate.NOM MODAL- break$_{trans}$ -PST
     'The ax "accidentally" broke the plate.' CMC
     (Consultant's comment: I can say this if I accidentally dropped the ax on the plate.)

(35) # Burç'uli-s tabaği   u-   t'rox   -u
       ax-DAT   plate.NOM 3.APPL- break$_{intrns}$ -PST
       Intended: 'The ax "accidentally" broke the plate.' OCC

Finally, there seems to be no requirement that the complement of the MODAL head has a change of state semantics. In fact, since it can combine with a voiceP, unergative verbs are also licensed, as shown by the examples in (36).

(36) a. Badi-k   barbal -u
        old.man-ERG speak   -PST
        'The old man spoke (≈ kept nagging).'

b. Badi-s   a-   barbal -u
   old.man-DAT   MODAL-   speak   -PST
   'The old man failed to keep himself from nagging.'

3.3   Interim Discussion

In the previous subsections, we have identified a number of syntactic contrasts between the two un-agentive constructions in Laz. Table 1 summarizes our findings.

Reflecting the respective analyses to be adopted for these constructions, the APPL and MODAL heads can have the meanings given in (37).

(37) a. $[\![\text{MODAL}]\!] = \lambda P_{\langle e, \langle v, t \rangle \rangle}. \lambda x. \forall w \in \text{CIRC}_{w^*} : \exists e\ [P(x)(e)\ \&\ e \text{ is in } w]$
   [to be revised]

   b. $[\![\text{APPL}]\!] = \lambda P_{\langle v, t \rangle}. \lambda x. \lambda e.\ P(e)\ \&\ \text{possessor}(e) = x$

It should be emphasized that the syntactic asymmetries in Table 1 do not follow from the meanings of the APPL and MODAL heads. Given that, we will also need to make use of syntactic selection to be able to encode what type of syntactic objects the APPL and MODAL heads can combine with.

Let us first see how the composition proceeds in OCC. This is shown in (38b) for the sentence in (38a).

(38) a. Bere-s   t'abaği   ⎡u⎤-   t'rox   -u
        child-DAT   plate.NOM   APPL.3   break$_{\text{intrns}}$ -PST
        'The child *accidentally* broke the plate.' OCC

TABLE 1   Compositional asymmetries between the two un-agentive constructions in Laz

	Oblique Causer Construction	Circumstantial Modal Construction
combines with anticausative VPs	✓	✗
combines with transitive VPs	✗	✓
combines with unergatives	✗	✓
co-occurs with overt causativizers	✗	✓
licenses inanimate oblique NPs	✗	✓

b. LF for (38a):

$\lambda e.\ break(e, plate)\ \&\ possessor(e)=child$

oblique causer$_{DAT}$ $\lambda x.\ \lambda e.\ break(e, plate)\ \&\ possessor(e)=x$

$\lambda P_{\langle v, t\rangle}.\ \lambda x.\ \lambda e.\ P(e)\ \&\ possessor(e)=x$ $\lambda e.\ break(e, plate)$
| |
APPL   VP

Given the composition in (38b), without the stipulation that the APPL syntactically selects for a VP (rather than a voiceP), it is not obvious what would rule out the ungrammatical sentence in (39a) where the APPL is combining with a voiceP.

(39) a. *Badi-s   bere-k   u-   bgar   -u
       old.man-DAT child-ERG   3.APPL-   cry   -PST
       Intended: 'The old man accidentally made the child cry.'

b. LF for (39a):

$\lambda e.\ cry(e)\ \&\ agent(e)=child\ \&$
$possessor(e)=old.man$

oblique causer$_{DAT}$ $\lambda x.\ \lambda e.\ cry(e)\ \&$
$agent(e)=child\ \&\ possessor(e)=x$

$\lambda P_{\langle v, t\rangle}.\ \lambda x.\ \lambda e.\ P(e)\ \&\ possessor(e)=x$ $\lambda e.\ cry(e)\ \&\ agent(e)=child$
| child
APPL   voice   VP

Now let us turn to the sample derivation for CMC, given in (40).

(40) a. Bere-s   t'abaği   a-   t'ax   -u
       child-DAT   plate.NOM   MODAL   break$_{trans}$ -PST
       'The child *accidentally* broke the plate.' CMC

TWO SEMANTIC PATHS TO UNINTENTIONAL CAUSATION

b. LF for (40a):

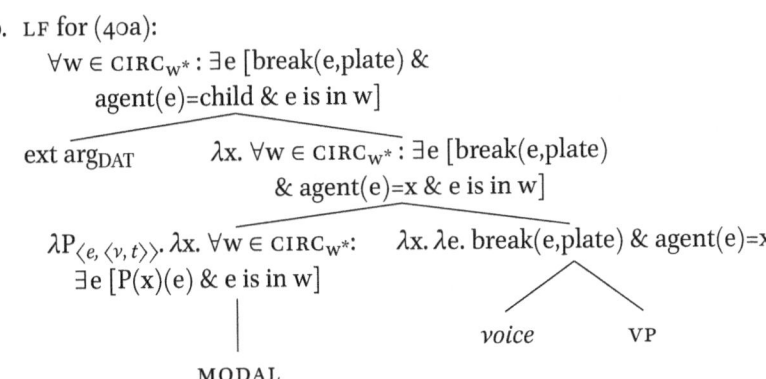

A similar overgeneration problem arises here unless we stipulate that the MODAL head combines with an unsaturated voiceP (rather than an unsaturated VP, i.e. a verb).

(41) a. *Oşk'uri-s a-   kts   -u
       apple-DAT MODAL- rot   -PST
       Intended: 'The apple *accidentally* got rotten.'

b. LF for (41a):

$\forall w \in \text{CIRC}_{w^*} : \exists e \, [\text{go.rotten}(e,\text{apple}) \, \& \, e \text{ is in } w]$

OBL NP$_{\text{theme}}$ $\lambda x. \forall w \in \text{CIRC}_{w^*} : \exists e \, [\text{go.rotten}(e,x) \, \& \, e \text{ is in } w]$

$\lambda P_{\langle e, \langle v, t \rangle \rangle}. \lambda x. \forall w \in \text{CIRC}_{w^*}:$ $\lambda x. \lambda e. \, \text{go.rotten}(e,x)$
$\exists e \, [P(x)(e) \, \& \, e \text{ is in } w]$ |
                              | V
                          MODAL

To close, the syntactic properties of OCC and CMC are consistent with the non-modal and modal analyses adopted for them, respectively. However, we have also seen that the meanings of APPL and MODAL that feature in OCC and CMC respectively do not suffice to derive their syntactic properties, calling for additional syntactic stipulations to prevent overgeneration. In the next section, we turn to the interpretational asymmetries between OCC and CMC, which provide evidence that the two constructions instantiate distinct semantic paths to the unintentional causation reading.

4 Interpretational Contrasts

In what follows, I show that OCC and CMC instantiate two distinct sets of meanings, supporting the idea that non-modal and modal paths to unintentional causation can co-exist in the grammar of a language. I discuss three types of data points. In section 4.1, I show that the set of meanings available to the Oblique Causer Construction is a proper subset of the meanings available to the Circumstantial Modal Construction. In other words, they don't exhibit the same 'polysemy' profiles. In section 4.2, I show that the two constructions when licensed to describe the same situation (unintentional causation) differ in the way the oblique NP is related to the change of state. In section 4.3, I discuss how the two constructions behave in downward entailing environments.

4.1 The Asymmetry in the Polysemy Profiles

The Oblique Causer Construction and the Circumstantial Modal Construction in Laz can both describe situations where the individual that the oblique NP refers to unintentionally leads to a change of state, as shown in (42).

(42) a. Ma   oşk'uri   do- m- i-   kts -u
     I.DAT apple.NOM PV- 1- APPL- rot -PST
     'I *accidentally* let the apple go rotten.' OCC

    b. Ma   oşk'uri   do- m- a-   kts -in   -u
     I.DAT apple.NOM PV 1- MODAL- rot -CAUS -PST
     'I *accidentally* let the apple go rotten.' CMC

Moreover, both constructions can felicitously describe a situation in which a change of state occurs after some effort or unexpectedly. Consider the scenario in (43) where both constructions are again felicitous.

(43) Context: A group of kids try to break a big stone. After multiple unsuccessful attempts, Arte tries for one last time, and unexpectedly the stone breaks. Arte, then, can utter:

    a. (didi kva)   m- i-   t'rox   -u!
     big stone.NOM 1- APPL- break$_{intrns}$ -PST
     'I managed to break it! (the big stone).' OCC

b. (didi kva)   m-   a-   t'ax   -u!
   big stone.NOM 1-   MODAL- break_trans -PST
   'I managed to break (it/the big stone)!' CMC

The parallelism between the two constructions is limited to these two shared readings. Importantly, there are readings that CMC can convey while OCC cannot.

The CMC can describe a dispreferred action that is taken intentionally. For example, in the context given in (44), there is an agentive intentional action seemingly forced by the circumstances and (44a) can report this action. The attempt to construct a parallel agentive action using the Oblique Causer Construction fails to give the intended meaning, as shown in (44b).

(44) Context: The beggar seemed genuinely in need and was very persistent. Although I didn't have a lot of money:

   a. Mak'vande-s para   me- m- a-   ç   -u
      beggar-to money.NOM   PV- 1- MODAL- give -PST
      'I couldn't not give money to the beggar.' CMC

   b. # Mak'vande-s para   me- m- i-   l   -u
        beggar-to money.NOM PV- 1- APPL-   go   -PST
        Intended: 'I couldn't not let the money go to the beggar.' OCC
        (✓ if the speaker fails to prevent their money falling and landing in the beggar's hand)

The contrast between CMC and OCC in the intentional yet dispreferred action context is more clear when the CMC variant builds on a causativized verb, which allows us to construct the OCC variant leaving out the overt causativizer. As shown in (45), while both OCC and CMC can describe an unintentional causation situation, only CMC is able report a change of state that was intentionally caused by an agent but was dispreferred by that agent.

(45) a. Ma   k'oğoni   do- m- a-   ğur   -in   -u
        I.DAT mosquito.NOM   PV- 1- MODAL- die   -CAUS -PST
        ✓ 'I accidentally killed the mosquito.' CMC
        ✓ 'I didn't prefer to kill the mosquito but I just had to.'

b. Ma   k'oğoni   do- m- i-   ğur -u
   I.DAT mosquito.NOM PV- 1-   APPL- die -PST
   ✓ 'I accidentally killed the mosquito.' OCC
   ✗ 'I didn't prefer to kill the mosquito but I just had to.'

Furthermore, all kinds of potentially agentive actions taken under *irresistible urge* can be expressed using the CMC, as shown in (46).

(46) a. Bere-s   çik'oleta   a-   şk'om -u
        child-DAT   chocolate.NOM   MODAL-   eat   -PST
        'The child couldn't but eat the chocolate.'

   b. Xordza-s   a-   dits'in -u
      woman-DAT   MODAL-   laugh   -PST
      'The woman couldn't but laugh.'

   c. Badi-s   a-   xval   -u
      old.man-DAT   MODAL-   cough -PST
      'The old man couldn't but cough.'

There is no way to build these sentences in the OCC, as shown in (47). This is predicted given that the verbs lack anticausative variants, leading to ungrammaticality under OCC.

(47) a. *Bere-s   çik'oleta   u-   şk'om -u
        child-DAT   chocolate.NOM   APPL.3-   eat   -PST
        Intended: 'The child couldn't but eat the chocolate.'

   b. *Xordza-s   u-   dits'in -u
      woman-DAT   APPL.3-   laugh   -PST
      Intended: 'The woman couldn't but laugh.'

   c. *Badi-s   u-   xval   -u
      old.man-DAT   APPL.3-   cough -PST
      Intended: 'The old man couldn't but cough.'

Finally, CMC in Laz (in fact most frequently) expresses *agentive ability* (e.g. complex events that require skill).

(48) a. Şana-s   coxo-muşi   a-   nç'ar -u
       Şana-DAT   name-3SG.POS   MODAL-   write -PST
       'Şana was able to write her name.' (Context: Şana is a 4-year-old.)

   b. Tanura-s   kapça   a-   t'iğan -u
      Tanura-DAT anchovy.NOM   MODAL-   fry   -PST
      'Tanura was able to fry the anchovies.'

   c. Biçi-s   puci   a-   nç'val -u
      boy-DAT   cow.NOM   MODAL-   milk   -PST
      'The boy was able to milk the cow.'

Syntactic restrictions on OCC again prevent building OCC variants of these sentences, as shown in (49).

(49) a. *Şana-s   coxo-muşi   u-   nç'ar -u
        Şana-DAT   name-3SG.POS APPL.3- write -PST
        Intended: 'Şana was able to write her name.' (Context: Şana is a 4-year-old.)

   b. *Tanura-s   kapça   u-   t'iğan -u
      Tanura-DAT anchovy.NOM   APPL.3- fry   -PST
      Intended: 'Tanura was able to fry the anchovies.'

   c. *Biçi-s   puci   u-   nç'val -u
      boy-DAT   cow.NOM   APPL.3- milk   -PST
      Intended: 'The boy was able to milk the cow.'

To summarize, the readings that OCC can express is a subset of the readings that CMC can express. I have tried to argue that this is not simply because of the syntactic differences between the two constructions. In particular, we are able to construct grammatical OCC and CMC pairs where only CMC is felicitous in dispreferred but intentional action context (while both are felicitous in unintentional/accidental action context). I take 'action under irresistible urge' and 'agentive ability' readings to be impossible in OCC, for syntactic restrictions on OCC prevent constructing these sentences grammatically. It should be noted that the readings that CMC can express are fully parallel to the set of readings Davis et al. (2009) report for St'át'imcets. Assuming that Davis et al. (2009) are right in their analysis of St'át'imcets facts, the range of meanings

CMC in Laz is able to express should also fall under circumstantial necessity and circumstantial possibility (Kratzer, 1989), suggesting that CMC does indeed involve a circumstantial modal.

4.2 The Asymmetry in What Role the Oblique NP Has

OCC and CMC in Laz both have an oblique/dative NP. As we have discussed, the way they relate to the events, however, are different. The oblique NP in CMC is just an external argument, as it semantically saturates the missing external argument slot of *voice*. What enables this is the denotation of the MODAL head. However, the oblique NP in the Oblique Causer Construction does not relate to the change of state event as an agent/external argument, but as a possessor according to the proposals in Cuervo (2003) and Schäfer (2008).

This asymmetry is detectable when the two constructions are felicitous in the same situation. As shown in (50) below, in a context where the two constructions are equally felicitous, there is a difference in the possibility of ascribing an *agentive credit* to the oblique NP. We can understand this to be the case because a denial of the agentive action, as in (50c), can be a follow-up to OCC in (50a), but not to CMC in (50b).

(50) Context: A group of kids try to break a big stone. After multiple unsuccessful attempts, Arte tries for one last time, and unexpectedly the stone breaks.

    a. Arte-s   didi   kva   *u-*   t'rox   -u
       Arte-DAT big stone.NOM 3.APPL- break$_{\text{intrns}}$ -PST
       'Arte managed to break the big stone.' OCC

    b. Arte-s   didi   kva   *a-*   t'ax   -u
       Arte-DAT big stone.NOM MODAL- break$_{\text{trans}}$ -PST
       'Arte was able to break the big stone.' CMC

    c. ... ama va   t'ax   -u
       but   NEG break$_{\text{trans}}$ PST
       '... Lit: but he didn't break it.' (≈ it wasn't him who broke it.)
       ✓ as a follow-up to (50a)
       ✗ as a follow-up to (50b)

I argue that the contrast reported here follows from the asymmetry in what role the oblique NP has in OCC and CMC. The oblique NP in (50b) is an external argument, whereas the oblique NP in (50a) is not. The sentence in (50c) cannot be a follow-up for the assertion in (50b) since the two statements are in contradiction. While (50b) asserts that Arte is the agent of a stone-breaking event, (50c) denies that. However, the oblique NP in OCC is not an external argument (neither an agent nor a causer). What (50a) says is along the lines of "When Arte gave it a shot, the stone broke", which does not directly give agentive credit to Arte as would presumably be predicted under the vague semantics of possession. Accordingly, the follow-up can be seen as reinforcing the implicature that Arte is *not* the agent.[18] Hence, this finding gives some plausibility to the idea that the vague possession semantics for the Oblique NP is the source of the unintentional causation inference.

4.3 The Asymmetry in Downward Entailing Environments

As we have seen examples of, CMC can be used to talk about agentive abilities as well as actions performed under compulsion/irresistible urge. Accordingly, many examples of this construction are perceived as ambiguous in appropriate pragmatic contexts. For example, (51) allows both a translation that features a possibility modal and a translation that features a necessity modal.

(51) Bere-s   çik'oleta   a-   şk'om   -u
     child-DAT   chocolate.NOM   MODAL-   eat   -PST
     'The child was able to eat the chocolate.' *circumstantial possibility*
     'The child couldn't but eat the chocolate.' *circumstantial necessity*

The example in (51) illustrates *force variability*. As Deal (2011) argues based on her careful study of a force variable modal in Nez Perce, force variability in some languages may be a consequence of the fact that there is no dual for a possibility modal (i.e. the corresponding necessity modal is missing in the language).[19] The idea is that due to entailment, a possibility claim is also true in a situation where the corresponding necessity claim would be true. In binary modal systems, a possibility claim generates the implicature that the corresponding necessity claim is false. However, when there is no dual for a possibility modal, no such implicature is derived, which makes it possible for speakers to make a possibility claim in a situation where a necessity claim would also be true.

---

18 My consultant paraphrases (50a) along with its follow-up in (50c) as follows: "When Arte gave it a shot, the stone broke but it wasn't really Arte who broke it."
19 See also section 2.5 in Kratzer (2012) for relevant discussion.

If the force variability observed with CMC in Laz fits this description, the modal in question should be a possibility modal, as in (52) (i.e. not a necessity modal or not a lexically force-ambiguous modal).

(52) $[\![\text{MODAL 'a-'}]\!] = \lambda P_{\langle e, \langle v, t \rangle \rangle}. \lambda x. \exists w \in \text{CIRC}_{w^*} : \exists e \, [P(x)(e) \, \& \, e \text{ is in } w]$
[final]

I argue that this is what we find in Laz. As Deal (2011) argues, in environments where entailment relations are reversed there should only be one construal because a possibility modal is stronger than its dual in such environments. For example, in the scope of negation, we should only find the not>possible reading, not the not>necessary reading. First, consider the deontic modal *o'qa* in Nez Perce, which can in appropriate contexts be translated into English with the possibility modal *can* or the necessity modal *must* as shown in (53a) and (53b). However, as (53c) shows, under negation, there is no ambiguity in the way it can be translated. The only interpretation (53c) has is the interpretation we expect to see if the modal is a possibility modal.

(53) a. tepelwéeku's-ne   'aa-p-ó'qa   hip-naaq'í-t-pa
      candy-OBJ   3OBJ-eat-MODAL   eat-finish-PART1-LOC
      'You *can* eat candy after the meal.'

     b. náqc-wa   hi-pa-'ác-o'qa
        one-HUM   3SUBJ-S.PL-enter-MODAL
        'People *must* go in one at a time.'

     c. wéet'u   'ee   kiy-ó'qa
        not   you   go-MODAL
        i. ✓ 'You cannot go.' [not-possible]
        ii. ✗ 'You do not have to go.' [not-necessary] (*Nez Perce*, Deal (2011): pp. 11, 12, 22)

The modal in CMC in Laz seems to be the same as *o'qa* in Nez Perce. As shown in (54), there is no ambiguity under negation. The same pattern is observed under a negated neg-raising predicate as shown in (55).

(54) Bere-s   çik'oleta   var   a-   şk'om   -u
    child-DAT   chocolate.NOM   NEG   MODAL-   eat   -PST
    ✓ 'It is not the case that the child was able to eat the chocolate.'
    ¬ > *circumstantial possibility*

    ✗ 'It is not the case that the child couldn't but eat the chocolate.'
    ¬ > *circumstantial necessity*

(55) [Bere-s   ist'ik'anepe   na=   a-   t'ax   -u]   va
    child-DAT   glasses.NOM   COMP=   MODAL-   break   -PST   NEG
    v-idușun-am
    1-think-IMPF
    ✓ 'I don't think the child was able to break the glasses.'
    ¬ > *circumstantial possibility*

    ✗ 'I don't think the child couldn't not break the glasses.'
    ¬ > *circumstantial necessity*

Hence, we systematically have the not-possible readings when the modal in CMC is in the scope of negation. This is the case even when a necessity construal would make more sense.

(56) Xordza-s   var   a-   dits'in   -u
    woman-DAT   NEG   MODAL-   laugh   -PST
    ✓ 'It is not the case that the woman was able to laugh.'
    ✗ 'It is not the case that the woman couldn't but laugh.'

As a matter of fact, the unavailability of the necessity construal for the modal in CMC is not limited to negation. It also extends to other downward-entailing environments. As shown in (57), CMC only permits the possibility construal in the antecedent of a conditional statement.

(57) g-   a-   dits'in   -en   -na,   nuk'u-sk'ani   imboni!
    2-   MODAL-   laugh   -IMPF   -COND,   face-your   wash.IMP.2SG!
    ✓ 'If you are able to laugh, wash your face!' (odd but available)
    ✗ 'If you cannot but laugh, wash you face!' (unavailable)

The systematic loss of force variability in downward entailing environments constitutes strong evidence in favor of adopting the modal analysis for CMC in Laz. Now the question is how negation affects the interpretation of the OCC in Laz.[20] As shown by the contrast between the examples in (58), there is an asymmetry between OCC and CMC with respect to change of state entailment under negation. CMC under negation has only one reading which entails the non-actuality of the change of state in Laz, as shown in (58a). However, OCC under negation can also be truthfully uttered when the change of state is actual but the oblique NP is asserted not to be related to the change of state. Hence, given the possibility of this reading, it does not entail that the change of state did not take place, as shown in (58b).[21]

(58) a. Arte-s kva var a- t'ax -u
Arte-DAT stone.NOM NEG MODAL- break$_{trns}$ -PST
'Arte was not able to break the stone.' CMC
⊨ the stone didn't break.

b. Arte-s kva var u- t'rox -u
Arte-DAT stone.NOM NEG 3.APPL- break$_{intrns}$ -PST
✓ 'When Arte tried to break it, the stone didn't break.' OCC
✓ 'The stone broke but Arte wasn't involved.'
⊭ the stone didn't break.

4.4 Summary of the Interpretational Contrasts

Table 2 below summarizes the interpretational asymmetries between CMC and OCC.

5 Summary of the Claims and Remaining Questions

In this paper, investigating two morphosyntactically distinct un-agentive constructions in Laz, I have shown that the proposed modal and non-modal analyses of unintentional causation inferences are both needed. While these two analyses have been proposed for un-agentive constructions in different languages, to the best of my knowledge, they have not been shown to co-exist in

---

[20] I was not able to get sound judgments on OCC in other downward entailing environments. Hence, I do not report the relevant data here.

[21] Admittedly, the contrast here is informative to the extent that we know why there is an actuality entailment (Bhatt, 1999) with the modal in the first place. Actuality entailments are outside the scope of this paper. For relevant discussion, see Hacquard (2006, 2020); Alxatib (2016); Nadathur (2020) among others.

TABLE 2 Interpretational asymmetries between CMC and OCC

	CMC	OCC
Readings:	✓	✓
– unintentional/accidental causation		
– (unexpectedly) manage-to	✓	✓
– dispreferred but intentional action	✓	✗
– action under irresistible urge	✓	N/A
– agentive ability requiring skills	✓	N/A
Agentive credit to oblique NP	✓	✗
Non-actuality of change of state entailed under negation	✓	✗

the same language, in a way that constitutes empirical evidence that grammar allows both paths. This paper has aimed to fill this gap.

We have documented that in Laz, one way to create the unintentional causation inference is OCC, in which an oblique NP combines with an anticausative change of state VP. This seems to attested widely in typologically different linguistic families (Fauconnier, 2011). The account Schäfer (2008) proposes for this construction, which I have adopted, posits an APPL head that relates the oblique NP to a change of state event as its possessor, building on Cuervo (2003). From the semantics associated with this morphosyntax, which is in competition with the canonical causative structures where the external argument is introduced by voice, speakers can infer that the possessor of the change of state has a source relation that is distinct from the canonical agent relation. In that way, the unintentional causation inference is derived as an implicature, as the canonical agent relation is, at least prototypically, intentional.

The second way to derive the unintentional causation inference involves a circumstantial necessity modal, as was argued in Davis et al. (2009) for St'át'imcets and in Rivero et al. (2010) for Polish. I have argued that what I labelled CMC in Laz instantiates this path, albeit indirectly using a circumstantial possibility modal lacking its dual. This is a pattern, distinct from the one we find St'át'imcets where the modal is reported to be a circumstantial necessity modal and exhibit force variability by a domain-narrowing mechanism using choice functions (Rullmann et al., 2008). It is also different from the parallel construction in Polish where the modal is again lexically a necessity modal but does not exhibit force variability. The idea that a possibility modal can be used in situations where a necessity claim would be true is predicted due to entailment, as Deal (2011) argues based on the force variable deontic possibility modal in Nez Perce, which lacks its dual. Hence, I argue that Laz instantiates this less studied and less documented modal path to the unintentional causation inference, using a circumstantial possibility modal. There is also anecdotal evidence that Laz speakers indeed use a circumstantial possibility modal to derive this inference. The Turkish sentence in (59), attested in a Facebook post by a Laz-Turkish bilingual, illustrates that this force variability pattern may even infiltrate their use of Turkish.[22] The intended interpretation, not available in Turkish, would require a circumstantial necessity modal, which Turkish has but Laz does not.

(59) Hata   yap-abil-di-m.   Ondan   beni   kov-du-lar.
     mistake   make-ABILITY-PST-1SG   that.from me   fire-PST-PL
     Lit: 'I was able to make a mistake. That's why they fired me.' Turkish
     Reading intended by the speaker: 'I unintentionally made a mistake. That's why they fired me.'

There are also remaining questions about the proposals adapted for CMC and OCC. For example, in the non-modal analysis, what exactly the possession semantics means in the context of events is not obvious. Without unpacking this relation, it is not straightforward to reason about how the unintentional causation implicature derives in competition with the canonical agent relation. Furthermore, it is not clear how to derive the syntactic restrictions on what APPL$_{possessive}$ head can combine with. Likewise, unresolved questions about circumstantial modals in general carry over to the modal analysis. For instance, plain circumstantial possibility does not quite capture the meaning of agentive ability ascriptions, cf. Hackl (1998). I refer the reader to relevant work: Mandelkern et al. (2017); Nadathur (2020); Schwarz (2020); Willer (2021, a.o.). Moreover, circumstantial modals often give rise to actuality entailments (Bhatt, 1999; Hacquard, 2020), which CMC in Laz exhibits under the perfective aspect, as shown in (60).[23] The phenomenon of actuality entailments and the linguistic representation of causation are potentially related. See Hacquard (2020) on actuality entailments and Nadathur (2020) for relevant discussion from the perspective of its interaction with causality.

---

[22] Almost all competent Laz speakers are Laz-Turkish bilinguals as schooling is only available in Turkish.

[23] The perfective outer aspect is morphologically zero but can be inferred when the overt imperfective aspect is absent.

(60) Arte-s   didi   kva   a-   t'ax   -u
    Arte-DAT   big   stone.NOM   MODAL- break$_{trans}$ -PST
    'Arte was able to break the big stone'
    ⊨ Arte broke the big stone.

My hope is that the empirical contribution of the current paper paves the way to a more thorough understanding of unintentional causation inferences and more generally on the interplay of intentionality, causality, and modality in natural languages.

References

Alxatib, Sam (2016). Actuality Entailments, Negation, and Free Choice Inferences. *Semantics and Linguistic Theory*, 26: 451–470.

Bhatt, Rajesh (1999). *Covert Modality in Non-finite Contexts*. PhD thesis, University of Pennsylvania.

Bruening, Benjamin (2013). By Phrases in Passives and Nominals. *Syntax*, 16(1): 1–41.

Copley, Bridget (2021). Reconciling Modal and Causal Representations for Salish Out of Control Forms. Proceedings of WCCFL39.

Cuervo, Maria Cristina (2003). *Datives at Large*. PhD thesis, MIT.

Davis, Henry, Matthewson, Lisa, and Rullmann, Hotze (2009). Out of Control Marking as Circumstantial Modality in St'át'imcets. In Hogeweg, Lotte, de Hoop, Helen, and Malchukov, Andrej L., editors, *Cross-linguistic Semantics of Tense, Aspect and Modality*. John Benjamins, Amsterdam.

Deal, Amy Rose (2009). The Origin and Content of Expletives: Evidence from "Selection". *Syntax*, 12(4): 285–323.

Deal, Amy Rose (2011). Modals without Scales. *Language*, 87: 559–585.

Demirok, Ömer (2013). AGREE as a Unidirectional Operation: Evidence from Laz. MA Thesis, Bogaziçi University.

Demirok, Ömer (2018). A Modal Approach to Dative Subjects in Laz. In Hucklebridge, Sherry and Nelson, Max, editors, *Proceedings of the Forty-Eighth Annual Meeting of the North East Linguistic Society*. CreateSpace Independent Publishing Platform.

Fauconnier, Stefanie (2011). Involuntary Agent Constructions Are Not Directly Linked to Reduced Transitivity. *Studies in Language*, 35(2): 311–336.

Ganenkov, Dmitry, Maisak, Timur, and Merdanova, Solmaz (2008). Non-canonical Agent Marking in Agul. In de Hoop, Helen and de Swart, Peter, editors, *Differential Subject Marking*. Kluwer, Dordrecht.

Hackl, Martin (1998). On the Semantics of "Ability Attributions". Unpublished Ms, MIT.

Hacquard, Valentine (2006). *Aspects of Modality*. PhD thesis, MIT.

Hacquard, Valentine (2020). Actuality Entailments. In *The Blackwell Companion to Semantics*. Wiley, Hoboken, NJ.

Haspelmath, Martin (1993). *A Grammar of Lezgian*. Mouton de Gruyter, Berlin.

Haviland, John (1979). Guugu Yimidhirr. In Dixon, R. M. W. and Blake, Barry J., editors, *Handbook of Australian Languages*, pp. 27–180. John Benjamins, Amsterdam.

Kittilä, Seppo (2005). Remarks on Involuntary Agent Constructions. *Word*, 56(3): 381–419.

Kratzer, Angelika (1989). An Investigation of the Lumps of Thought. *Linguistics and Philosophy*, 12(5): 607–653.

Kratzer, Angelika (1996). Severing the External Argument from the Verb. In Rooryck, J. and Zarin, L., editors, *Phrase Structure and the Lexicon*. Kluwer, Dordrecht.

Kratzer, Agelika (2005). Building Resultatives. In Maienborn, Claudia and Wöllstein, Angelika, editors, *Event Arguments: Foundations and Applications*, pp. 177–212. Max Niemeyer Verlag, Tübingen.

Kratzer, Angelika (2012). *Modals and Conditionals: New and Revised Perspectives*. Oxford University Press.

Mandelkern, Matthew, Schultheis, Ginger, and Boylan, David (2017). Agentive Modals. *The Philosophical Review*, 126(3): 301–343.

McIntyre, Andrew (2006). The Interpretation of German Datives and English Have. In Hole, Daniel, Meinunger, André, and Abraham, Werner, editors, *Datives and Other Cases*, pp. 185–211. John Benjamins Publishing Company, Amsterdam.

Nadathur, Prerna (2019). *Causality, Aspect, and Modality in Actuality Inferences*. PhD thesis, Stanford University.

Nadathur, Prerna (2020). Causality and Aspect in Ability, Actuality, and Implicativity. Joseph Rhyne, Kaelyn Lamp, Nicole Dreier, Chloe Kwon, editors, *Proceedings of Semantics and Linguistic Theory (SALT) 30*. Linguistic Society of America.

Öztürk, Balkız (2013). Low, High and Higher Applicatives. In Camacho-Taboada, Victoria, Fernández, Ángel L. Jiménez, Martín-González, Javier, and Reyes-Tejedor, Mariano, editors, *Linguistik Aktuell/Linguistics Today* 197, pp. 275–296. John Benjamins.

Öztürk, Balkız and Pöchtrager, Markus (2011). *Pazar Laz*. LINCOM, München.

Pylkkänen, Liina (2002). *Introducing Arguments*. PhD thesis, MIT.

Rivero, Mara Luisa, Arregui, Ana, and Frckowiak, Ewelina (2010). Variation in Circumstantial Modality: Polish versus St'át'imcets. *Linguistic Inquiry*, 41: 705–714.

Rullmann, Hotze, Matthewson, Lisa, and Davis, Henry (2008). Modals as Distributive Indefinites. *Natural Language Semantics*, 16: 317–357.

Schäfer, Florian (2008). *The Syntax of (Anti-)causatives. External Arguments in Change-of-State Contexts*. John Benjamins, Amsterdam.

Schäfer, Florian (2009). The Oblique Causer Construction across Languages. In Schardl, Anisa, Walkow, Martin, and Abdurrahman, Muhammad, editors, *Proceedings of the Thirty-Eighth Annual Meeting of the North East Linguistic Society*. CreateSpace Independent Publishing Platform.

Schwarz, Wolfgang (2020). "Ability and Possibility". *Philosophers' Imprint*, 20(6): 1–21.

Willer, Malte (2021). Two Puzzles about Ability *can*. *Linguistics and Philosophy*, 44: 551–586.

Letting Structure Speak with Authority: Constraining Agents' Choices with French *laisser*

Marta Donazzan
Nantes Université/LLING, France
marta.donazzan@univ-nantes.fr

Clémentine Raffy
Université Côte d'Azur, France, Universität zu Köln, Germany
clementine.raffy@gmail.com

Bridget Copley
CNRS and Université Paris 8/SFL, France
bridget.copley@cnrs.fr

Klaus von Heusinger
Universität zu Köln, Germany
klaus.vonheusinger@uni-koeln.de

Abstract

Agents' actions and intentions can be prompted or hindered in multiple ways. Across languages, verbs that lexicalize the causative primitives of CAUSE, ENABLE or PREVENT (Wolff & Song 2003) can help us understand the nature of agency, precisely because they involve multiple participants which are sometimes seen as being in a position of influencing each other via different types of relations. In this paper, we focus on the role of authority, intended as an influence that affects the choices available to a free agent with respect to the actions in service of their goal. We show that, while many causative verbs seem to imply the type of force relation between the participants in their lexical meaning, the French causative verb *laisser* is underspecified: the type of influence exerted by the two participants in a *laisser* relation is determined by the syntactic structure of the causative construction.

Keywords

causation – authority – agency – alternatives – free choice

1 Introduction

The French verb *laisser* 'let' is well-known for being peculiar among causative verbs in Romance, as it licenses two different embedded clauses. The sentence in (1) exemplifies the so-called infinitive construction, where *laisser* embeds an infinitive clause with a preverbal subject; in (2), the verb enters a complex predicate construction, which has received different analyses in the literature (e.g., Alsina 1992, Guasti 1996, Folli & Harley 2007). In this construction, the understood subject of the infinitive verb is realised postverbally, or, in the case of transitive verbs, as the complement of a preposition.[1]

(1) Jean a laissé les enfants manger.
    John laisser.PF the children eat.INF
    'John let the children eat.'

(2) Jean a laissé manger les enfants.
    John laisser.PF eat.INF the children
    'John let the children eat.'

The first question that arises with regards to (1) and (2) concerns the relation between form and meaning. It has been observed very early on (Borel 1972, Kayne 1975) that the two structures in (1) and (2) are correlated with two slightly different interpretations, but this intuition has been developed quite informally, and judgements are therefore not consistent in the literature, where the interpretive difference has been described as, at best, a pragmatic effect (Abeillé et al. 1997). We believe, however, that the relation between form and meaning deserves a more careful investigation, since differences in meaning can reflect differences in structure particularly in the case of causative constructions, where distinct interpretations correspond to different causative relations that are conceptualised in different ways. The link between syntax and conceptual structure is given by grammar, to the extent that grammar determines the way in which the participants in a causal relation are realised

---

1 For the purpose of this paper, we will discuss only examples where the embedded verb is intransitive, as, in many cases, speakers disprefer a post-verbal Causee in *laisser*-causatives with an embedded transitive verb such as (i.b) below:
(i) a. Jean a laissé les enfants détruire le château de sable.
    b. ?Jean a laissé détruire le château de sable aux enfants.
    'Jean let the children destroy the sandcastle.'
The reader is addressed to the aforementioned literature for more detailed analyses of the syntax of complex predicate constructions in French and in Romance languages.

as the arguments of a causative predicate. As has been extensively discussed in the literature (see e.g. Shibatani 1976) the grammars of different languages deal with conceptual structure in different ways, and there may be alternative ways of realising causal chains even within one particular language. One of the most famous examples is probably the distinction between direct and indirect causation as expressed by lexical (3a) vs. analytical constructions (3b) in English (Fodor 1970). It is generally assumed that the lexical causative verb *kill* in English expresses a relation of direct causation, i.e. in (3a) John did something that directly led to the death of Bill. Causative constructions like *cause to die* in (3b), on the other hand, may also express a more indirect relation: John might have done something which started a longer causative chain leading, at the end, to the death of Bill (but see Neeleman & van de Koot 2012 for arguments against this generalisation).

(3) a. John killed Bill.
　　b. John caused Bill to die.

It is thus fairly reasonable to assume that the grammatical constructions in (1) and (2) may each realise a distinct causative relation.

In the specific case of (1) and (2), however, probing the issue of form and meaning leads to a related question, which is the main focus of this paper. Following the intuitions of native speakers, also reported in previous literature, the two interpretations can be paraphrased as such: while (1) can only convey that Jean had the intention to let the children eat, (2) seems to be also compatible with a scenario in which Jean is less directly responsible for their action, and merely failed to prevent them from eating. Looking at the interpretations, then, one may wonder: how are concepts such as intentions and causal responsibility expressed in language, or, more specifically, to what extent does grammar "see" intentions and map them into syntactic structures? The question is vast and goes far beyond grammatical analysis; we shall be satisfied if we manage to take a few steps towards an answer.[2]

In this paper, we show that the analysis of *laisser* may help us do so. To start with, we show that the distinct interpretations of the *laisser* constructions in (1) and (2) can be probed by looking at the particular type of influence that

---

[2] This vast domain includes several important questions for linguistics, such as the question of how competition of causative verbs in a single language affects their meanings, an issue that would require a comparative examination of causative configurations with different verbs (see Lauer & Nadathur 2018). Interesting also is the existence of *have*-causatives which can have authoritative meaning (Bjorkman & Cowper 2013, Copley 2018).

the subject of *laisser* (the Causer) exerts on the subject of the infinitive (the Causee). More specifically, in (1), but not in (2), this influence must be that of authority: sentence (1) represents a state of affairs that is compatible with a situation where John allows the children to eat by virtue of his position of authority – in other words, John authorises them to eat. This is not necessarily the case in (2), which is compatible with a situation where the children started to eat without being granted permission, and John merely did not intervene. The link between form and structure is intuitively the following: since authority can arguably be exerted only by intentional agents on intentional agents, and agentive thematic positions are constrained by grammar across languages, one can predict that authority-related interpretations may also be restricted to specific syntactic structures, i.e. the ones where the two participants are both mapped onto agentive positions. We claim that this is what determines the structural difference in the two French sentences. Evidence from French may in this sense support the hypothesis that these constructions are compositional, and that their structure is informative about meaning. In these constructions, both the syntax and the causative semantics are poorly understood. Thus, although we do not provide a full theory of the syntax-semantics interface for these constructions, our progress in making the semantics explicit goes a good deal of the way towards a fuller understanding of the syntactic structure. In section 4, we will make a nod at the kinds of structures that are suggested by our semantics, so as to show a possible starting point for future work.

The paper is organised as follows. In section 2, we expound on the theoretical assumptions that form the background of our analysis of the interpretation of causal relations as conceptual configurations. We draw these assumptions from recent approaches to the use of force-dynamic representations for meaning, as first proposed by Talmy (1983, 1988, 2000), developed by Wolff (2003, 2007), and further elaborated at the interface with linguistics by Copley & Harley (2015). In section 3, we discuss more specifically the formal representations of agency and authority in such configurations, and we come back to the case of *laisser* in section 4, where we show that looking at authority and intentions provides a solution to the interpretation issue raised above. Section 5 concludes.

2   Theoretical Background

2.1   *Causal Configurations in Force Theory*

Cognitive linguist Leonard Talmy first brought linguistic attention to the usefulness of force-dynamic representations for natural language semantics

(Talmy 1983, 1988, 2000, e.g.; see also Copley 2019 for an overview). The idea we are interested in here is the grounding of the concept of causation in people's cognitive representations, focussing in particular on the representation of forces and their interactions in space (Wolff & Thorstad 2016). We follow Wolff and Song 2003, Wolff 2007 in specifying how the concept of CAUSE, a primitive operator in lexical and syntactic decompositional approaches (see, a.o., Dowty 1979, Hale & Keyser 1993, Ramchand 2008), may be deconstructed into finer elements, and how these elements can be represented in a formal system interacting with grammar. In this section, we will start by reviewing the basic configurations predicted by Wolff and Song's theory, and give a quick review of the configurations that possibly underlie the meaning of different causative verbs. With this in mind, we will then be able to show how *laisser*, as a particular type of causative operator, may help us refine the set of primitives needed in structural representations of causation.

A causal configuration, for Wolff and Song, implies the interaction of an Agent and a Patient, represented as vector forces of given magnitude directed towards a goal. This type of conceptual representation gives rise at the level of individual configurations of forces, to three main causal concepts: CAUSE, ENABLE (which includes ALLOW and HELP) and PREVENT. The three concepts can be differentiated via three parameters, as detailed in Table 1: (i) the tendency of the Patient towards the goal – that is, whether the Patient's force is directed towards the endstate prior to the intervention of the Agent; (ii) the relationship between the tendencies of Agent or Patient – whether the two participants in the causal relation are both directed towards the goal or not; and (iii) the direction of the configuration – whether the goal is indeed targeted as the result of the interaction of the Agent's and Patient's forces. The dynamics of CAUSE, ENABLE and PREVENT can be represented as configuration of forces as in, respectively, Figures 1a, 1b and 1c, where the vector A represents the force associated with the Agent, P the force associated with the Patient, and R represents the position of the Patient as a result of their interaction.

TABLE 1 Representation of causal concepts (adapted from Wolff & Song 2003:284)

	Tendency of the patient for the result	Opposition of agent and patient	Occurrence of the result
CAUSE	no	yes	yes
ENABLE	yes	no	yes
PREVENT	yes	yes	no

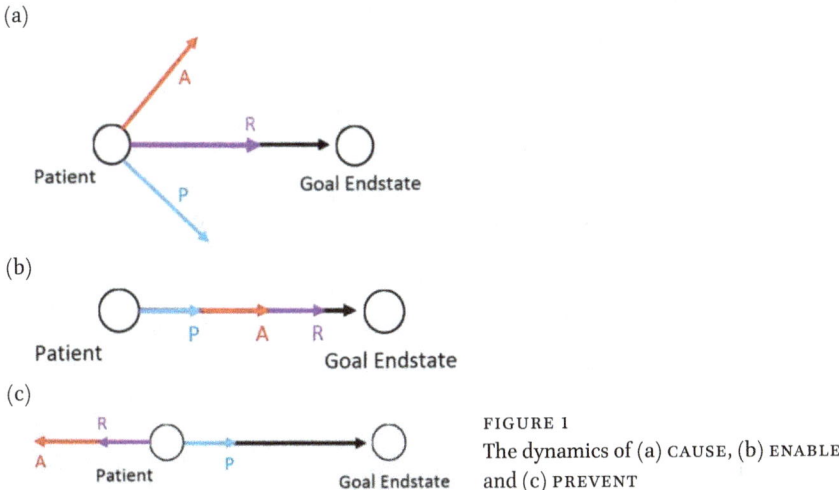

FIGURE 1
The dynamics of (a) CAUSE, (b) ENABLE and (c) PREVENT

One of the consequences of representing causal relations in vector space as in Figure 1 is that the goal does not need to be reached in order for a causal interaction to occur – the occurrence of the goal endstate depends on the magnitude and direction of the resultant vector. Therefore, according to the theory, one may predict that only CAUSE and ENABLE configurations are compatible with the actual occurrence of the goal endstate (since in the PREVENT configuration the R vector is not directed towards the goal); however, the occurrence of one of these two causal configurations does not guarantee by itself that the goal occurs. As we will see, this prediction is borne out in the case of *laisser*, which realises a particular case of the ENABLE configuration.

2.2 Types of Influences

The framework of this force-dynamic theory, in defining at least three possible causal configurations, also makes room for the hypothesis that the type of force interaction between Causer and Causee may correlate with the choice of different causative verbs lexicalising the relation. In the following, we would like to submit that lexicalisation may depend not only, more broadly, on the type of configuration (thus differentiating, in English, between the CAUSE, ENABLE and PREVENT configurations and the homonymous verbal predicates), but it can also be sensitive, more specifically, to some of the parameters that determine such configurations. One of these parameters, which we wish to discuss in detail, has to do with the type of influence that the Causer exerts on the Causee.

Throughout this paper, we use the term "influence" as a *porte-manteau* for different types of forces, starting from Talmy's observation that Causers can indeed exert pressure of various kinds: besides physical forces, intentions and social or psychological pressures can also influence the progression of an event towards an endstate (Wolff 2007).

In the case of LET verbs such as *laisser*, the type of influence is generally an intention.³ This is what seems to discriminate between *laisser* and other causative verbs realising ENABLE configurations in French, such as *permettre* 'allow'. The subject of *permettre* can exert either a psychological or a physical influence on the Causee. Accordingly, the sentence in (4a) may be interpreted in both ways: (4a) could mean that Marie authorised Julie to go out with her friends, or that, for example, she helped her climb out of a hole by joining her physical strength to hers. Authority cannot be at stake in (4b), where the wind enables the windmills to turn by exerting a purely physical force against their blades.

(4) a. Marie a permis à Julie de sortir.
Marie allow.PF to Julie to go-out
'Marie allowed Julie to go out/ Marie helped Julie go out.'

b. Le vent a permis aux éoliennes de tourner.
the wind allow.PF to-the windmills to turn
'The wind allowed the windmills to turn.'

---

3 In fact, *laisser* permits a few inanimate subjects with very particular complements, as in (i):
(i) Les rideaux laissent entrer la lumière du soleil.
the curtains laisser.PR enter the light of-the sun
'The curtains let the sunlight come in.'
The existence of a few idiosyncratic inanimate exceptions here meets Copley's (2018) criterion for "dispositional causation", where intentions are understood as a species of disposition. Intention involves, at the very least, an intender y who holds an intentional state e bearing some intentional relation toward an eventuality description p, such that, if all else is equal, an eventuality e' of that description occurs. The nature of the intentional relation could be understood as a preferential relation, where the state is some kind of preference for p, as in Heim (1992); or a dispositional relation, where the intentional state is defined as some kind of disposition to cause an eventuality that meets the eventuality description (as done explicitly in Portner 1997; somewhat implicitly in Condoravdi & Lauer 2009; and more explicitly in Condoravdi & Lauer 2012; 2016; Grano 2017). If the intentionality implicated in cases like (i) involved (only) preferences, then it would be mysterious why these inanimate exceptions are allowed to occur, as inanimate entities do not have preferences. If we view intentions as a kind of disposition, the inanimate exceptions can be those which have a relevant disposition that under certain circumstances causes the eventuality. The felicitous cases such as (i) might then be seen as involving a disposition of the subject that causes an event of the kind described by the complement, whereas those that do not admit *laisser* should be seen as describing impossible courses of events, where there is no such disposition of the subject that can cause an event of the kind described by the complement. See also Donazzan & Tovena (2016), who make a similar case for dispositions licensing a causative entailment in light-verb constructions.

LETTING STRUCTURE SPEAK WITH AUTHORITY   95

Laisser could be compared to *permettre* in its interpretation of authorisation in sentence (5a); however, (5a) lacks the second possible interpretation of (4a), where Marie would help Julie out of a hole. The fact that in the case of *laisser* the influence can only be an intention is also confirmed by the infelicity of (5b):

(5) a. Marie a laissé   Julie sortir.
       Marie allow.PF   Julie go-out
       'Marie let Julie go out.'

    b. #Le vent   a laissé   les   éoliennes   tourner.
       the wind laisser.PF   the   windmills   turn

We will see that intention must characterise both Causer and Causee when it takes the form of an authorisation from the Causer, as in (5a). This leaves us with the issue of characterising the role of the Causee as an intentional agent. We discuss this point in the next section, where we provide the first sketch of a formal representation of agency in causative structures.

3 Characterising Authority as a Constraint on Choice

We have seen that Marie in (5a) exerts a particular influence through an intentional act (an act that Marie performs because of her intention). Our aim in this section is to define more precisely the conceptual status of influences based on intention, and more specifically of the influence exerted by authority, and its effect within a causal chain. In accordance with our assumption that there exists a link between conceptual representations and language realisations, we will try to represent it in the grammatical structure by making use of tools provided by a formal framework.

3.1 *Agency as Choice*

Given that, as we have seen in the preceding section, authority is an influence exerted by agents, we start by providing a more general definition of agency. Along with standard philosophical literature (e.g. Anscombe 1957), we assume that agents have intentions when their action is directed towards a goal. We may then represent an intentional action as an influence that is directed towards the occurrence of a particular state of affairs; we represent formally this state of affairs as a proposition. What is important for our present concern is the observation that, when their will is unimpeded, agents have the choice of pursuing different goals. Following our initial assumption, then, these different goals will be represented as a set of alternative propositions. The signature of free agents is then that they have a choice over an ALT set of alternative propositions.[4]

Let's consider some examples. A sentence like (6) below is understood as depicting a situation where John's actions or will are directed towards realising a state of affairs in which he plays the piano.

(6) a. John intends to play the piano.
    b. John intend [John play the piano]
    c. ALT$_{JOHN}$:= {*play the piano*, ¬ *play the piano*}

Accordingly, let's assume that the goal of John may be represented by the proposition embedded under the predicate of intention. Alternative propositions are to be denoted, in linguistic expressions, by (non-tensed) clauses (Rooth 1992). Once the co-reference of the subject under the control configuration has been resolved, we may assume that the embedded clause in (6) denotes the proposition p, which in this case is *John play the piano*.

Since John is the holder of an intention and therefore an intentional agent, in principle he has the choice whether to pursue this goal or not: his choice includes a set of propositions alternative to p. In the absence of prominent focus on one of the elements in the embedded clause,[5] we take this set of alternatives to be the verum focus set of alternatives, namely p and $\neg p$. We represent alternative propositions as belonging to the set ALT, which minimally includes the proposition p expressed by the infinitive predicate (the prevalent) and a proposition $\neg p$, which is intended as a negation of the prevalent p (*John play the piano*).

The set of alternative states of affairs available to John may thus include other states of affairs, but the main predicate of the sentence states that John himself has restricted his choice to one possible alternative, that of playing the piano. In this sense, the matrix predicate, in complex constructions,

---

[4] The representation of choice from among a set of alternatives is meant to be fairly catholic and to be portable to any more sophisticated theory of intention of the reader's choice. All that we are representing here is choice within a set of alternatives, which is a necessary part of an adequate analysis of intention, however it is modeled (e.g., via preferences, beliefs, actions, properties; see Grano 2015, 2017 and references therein).

[5] Narrow focus on a constituent in the embedded clause seems to create other alternative sets in the usual manner: e.g., *Mary let John give a book to JILL* evokes a different alternative set from *Mary let John give A BOOK to Jill*. In the former, Mary constrains who John can give a book to, removing e.g. *John give a book to Bill* and *John give a book to Sue* from the John's alternative set {*John give a book to x*}, while in the latter, Mary constrains what John can give to Jill, removing, e.g., *John give a newspaper to Jill, John give a sandwich to Jill* from John's alternative set {*John give x to Jill*}.

determines how the ALT set is dealt with. As shown by the second conjunct in (7b), when the main predicate is not a causative verb or a modal operator, John, as a free agent, can choose to follow any other alternative goal which may be available to him.

(7) a. We asked John [to play the piano]
    ALT$_{JOHN}$:= $\{p, \neg p\}$
   b. We asked John to play the piano, but he watched TV instead.

Within a causal configuration, then, an influence affects the available choices of a free agent with respect to the actions in service of their goal(s). What happens when an influence is exerted by a free agent on another free agent, as in complex causative structures? More specifically, to what extent does the influence lexicalised by a specific causative predicate constrain the choices available to an agentive Causee?

3.2 Constraining Agency in Complex Causatives

The result of an influence can be conceived as the Causer's *preference* for one choice – that is, one course of action – among alternative options (Staraki 2017). Let's consider, for instance, sentence (8). In (8), contrary to (7) above, John's alternatives are reduced, and this follows from the influence exerted by Peter – John may want to play the piano or not, but Peter leaves him with no choice by setting the value of the ALT set to one possible state of affairs, represented by p. Therefore, adding the second conjunct in (8b) yields an infelicitous sentence.

(8) a. Peter forced John to play the piano.
    ALT$_{JOHN}$:= $\{p, \neg p\}$
    Peter sets value of ALT$_{JOHN}$:= $\{p\}$
   b. #Peter forced John to play the piano, but John didn't (play the piano).

In the semantic representation of causative constructions, we therefore model the influence required by the causative verb as the ability to constrain in different ways the set of alternative actions available to the lower agent (the Causee). Sentences (9) and (10) below represent causative configuration of the ENABLE and PREVENT type, respectively.

(9) Lucy allowed Peter to go out tonight.
    ALT$_{PETER}$:= $\{go\ out,\ not\ go\ out\}$
    Lucy sets value of ALT$_{PETER}$:= $\{go\ out,\ not\ go\ out\}$

(10) John prevented Mark from watching TV.
 ALT$_{MARK}$ {*watch TV, not watch TV*}
 John sets value of ALT$_{MARK}$:= {*not watch TV*}

The representation in (9) captures the intuition that the Causer in ENABLE configurations exerts an influence that is in accordance with the tendency of the Causee (see also Table 1); therefore, all possible choices are granted. In (10), the influence of the Causer is directed against the Causee's tendency, and therefore the value of ALT is set to {¬p}.

So much for the different configurations. However, we have seen that influences can be of different types, and that we may assume, following a lexicalisation hypothesis, that certain causative predicates impose constraints on the nature of the relevant influence. For example, the English verb *forbid* in (11) is a predicate that, as a causative predicate of the PREVENT type, requires the Causer to exert an influence on the Causee. Contrary to *prevent*, however, *forbid* requires two agentive arguments, and imposes additional constraints on the type of influence exerted by the Causer. More specifically, the proposition realised by (11) is felicitous only in a situation where God may exert a type of authority over Adam: Adam may want to eat the apple or not, but God, who has authority over him, sets the value of Adam's alternative set to {¬p}. Crucially, however, as is well-known given the actual outcome, it is still acceptable for the Causee in (11) to overcome the Causer's influence and exercise his free will.

(11) God forbade Adam to eat the apple (but Adam did eat the apple).

Authority is then a type of coercive intention that acts as a force constraining an intentional agent's choice of action. Contrary to physical force, however, authority is not strictly implicative (the free agent may still have a choice) and is legitimate only if the two agents are in a social or contextual relation that justifies the influence itself.[6] In case of mismatch in the presupposed authority relation, verbs of influence such as *forbid* are infelicitous, cf. (12a) vs. (12b).

(12) a. The judge forbade the defendant to speak.
 b. #The defendant forbade the judge to speak.

---

6 The authority relation is presupposed, but of course, as in (11) above, it may turn out that the Causer did not have the ability to decide what happens after all; see Copley (2008) for discussion of this idea.

4 When Syntax Matters: Structural Constraints on Authority Relations

The French causative verb *laisser* 'let' is generally described as realizing an ENABLE relation (as defined in Wolff & Song 2003, cf. Table 1). As we have seen in section 1, contrary to other ENABLE verbs such as English *let*, *laisser* can embed its complement clause in two ways. Unlike their English translation, then, the two structures, exemplified here by (13a) and (13b), are said to correlate with two interpretations (Borel 1972, Kayne 1975).

(13) a. Le gardien a laissé   le   prisonnier s'échapper. *Pre-v Causee*
       the guard   laisser.PF the prisoner   CL-escape
       'The guard let the prisoner escape.'

   b. Le gardien a laissé   s'échapper le   prisonnier. *Post-v Causee*
       the guard   laisser.PF CL-escape the prisoner
       'The guard let the prisoner escape.'

Discussing specifically the examples in (13), Kayne (1975: 222) remarks that the structure (13a), where the Causee is realised preverbally, can be interpreted as a situation where the guard acted with "complicity" or "deliberate neglect" with respect to the prisoner's attempt to escape, while there is no such inference in (13b). In other words, we may say that (13a) carries an intentional flavour: it seems to be the guard's intention to give the prisoner the choice to escape.

Following our analysis, then, only (13a) implies an influence that can be characterised as an intention. But how does this conceptual interpretation correlate with the structural difference between the two sentences? And what is the influence exerted by the guard in (13b)?

In the following, we will address this question by looking at the constraints on interpretation imposed on both the pre-v and the post-v constructions. For the sake of clarity, we will set up a context where the two participants are quite uncontroversially in an authority relation. We take as a prototypical case, among other possibilities, the relation of a judge and a defendant in court, assuming that the authority of the judge is recognised and enforced by the law. Also, in order to highlight the desired interpretations, we will make use of specific contextual conditions: if the Causer authorises the Causee to act, we may expect that the Causee's action will necessarily start after the authorisation is granted. Conversely, if the Causer merely does not interfere with the Causee's action, it may be possible that their action is already going on, and the Causer just refrains from intervening.

4.1 Authority and Preverbal Causee

As we have seen in the preceding section, we may characterise authority relations as implying the presence of two intentional agents, one of which, the Causer, performs an intentional act that constrains the choice of action available to the Causee.

With this in mind, let's consider sentence (14).

(14) La salle d'audience était silencieuse. Finalement. ...
      The courtroom was silent. Eventually ...
      La   juge   a laissé   l'accusé   parler
      the   judge laisser.PF   the-defendant   speak
      'The judge let the defendant speak.'

The context for sentence (14) enhances the authority reading – the judge has authority on the defendant, and the defendant's action, as evidenced by the preceding sentence, is due to start only after the authorisation has been granted. More importantly, we predict that the sentence should only be compatible with a situation where the Causer is in a position of authority with respect to the Causee: similarly to the *forbid* case discussed with respect to example (12), we expect such structures to be infelicitous if the higher agent has no authority over the lower one. This prediction is borne out: sentence (15), which, if we are correct, displays a mismatch in the authority relation, is considered unnatural or degraded in a prototypical courtroom context by most of the native speakers we have consulted.[7]

(15) La salle d'audience était silencieuse. Finalement ...
      The courtroom was silent. Eventually ...
      ??l'accusé   a laissé   parler la juge
      the-defendant   laisser.PF   speak the judge

How is this interpretation related to the syntactic structure of the sentence? According to the representation that we have adopted so far, the verb *laisser* embeds a proposition whose non-tensed predicate is *parler* 'speak'. The Causee

---

7 Note however that the constraint here is structural, and not lexically enforced as in the case of predicates such as *forbid* (or *authorise*), which express authority as part of their meaning. This may be the reason for the difference in acceptability between (12b) and (15) among native speakers, for whom the feeling of infelicity for sentence (15) is weaker than that for sentence (12b), and a context is needed in order to make the contrast more salient.

is understood as the agentive subject of the embedded verb, i.e. the lower agent of the causal relation.

The lower agent, being an intentional subject, introduces in the formal representation an ALT set (16b) whose members are the prevalent p (*speak*) and its negation $\neg p$. The meaning of *laisser*, as a causative verb, is that the higher agent must be able to restrict the ALT set with authority. Recall however that, if we are right in considering *laisser* an ENABLE verb, the Causer is acting in accordance with the Causee's tendency, and therefore both alternatives in ALT are made available to the Causee (16c).

(16) a. laisser [$_{VoiceP}$ the defendant [$_{vP}$ speak]]
 b. ALT$_{defendant}$:= {*speak, not speak*}
 c. Judge sets the value of ALT$_{defendant}$:= {*speak, not speak*}

This prediction is borne out: *laisser* is not an implicative verb, the fact that the Causee's tendency is directed towards the goal does not imply that the goal is eventually reached. We may qualify the projection of the outcome as an implicature, as the continuation in (17) seems to confirm.

(17) La juge a laissé l'accusé parler, mais
 the judge laisser.PF the-defendant speak.INF but
 il est resté muet.
 he remain.PF silent
 'The judge let the defendant speak, but he kept silent.'

4.2 Causation by Omission: Postverbal Causee

Let's consider now the interpretation of the postverbal construction, exemplified here by (18).

(18) La juge a laissé parler l'accusé.
 the judge laisser.PF speak.INF the-defendant
 'The judge let the defendant speak.'

We claim that post-v constructions like (18) do not necessarily make reference to an authority relation and thus do not trigger the interpretation of the Causer as an influencer. Since the relation is not one of authority, we predict that no mismatch in authority can ever arise; indeed, native speakers' judgements confirm this prediction, as (19) is judged more acceptable in a normal courtroom situation than (15) above.

(19) L'accusé a laissé parler la juge.
the-defendant laisser.PF speak.INF the judge
'The defendant let the judge speak.'

In postverbal constructions, the lower subject is not interpreted as an external argument of the embedded verb, it is not realised as an agentive subject, and therefore no ALT set is introduced.

In some sense, the sentence may be interpreted as a case of enabling by omission: i.e. as describing a situation where the higher agent does not exert any influence in order to restrict the lower subject's action.

Although the exact characterisation of the syntactic structure of pre-v and post-v constructions is beyond the scope of this paper, the pre- or post-v position of the embedded subject may be correlated to distinct realisations of the argument structure of the embedded predicate. Following standard assumptions in the literature (Kratzer 1996, Harley 2013, Alexiadou et al. 2015, a.o.), we may suppose that the agentive subject of the infinitive is introduced as the specifier of a dedicated functional projection, such as VoiceP (20a), of which, following our analysis, we would give the tentative denotation in (20a). The post-v complement, on the other hand, would be a vP without external argument position (20b).

(20) a. Preverbal complement: $[\![\text{VoiceP}]\!] = \lambda s \, . \, \text{chooser}(x, s, \text{ALT}\,([\![\text{vP}]\!]))$
  & $\text{agent}(x, e)\, \& \,[\![\text{vP}]\!](e)$
 b. Postverbal complement: $[\![\text{vP}]\!] = \lambda e \, . \, [\![\text{vP}]\!](e)$

What ultimately happens to these denotations in the syntactic derivation may be more complex and is beyond the scope of this paper. In the following section, we will discuss some additional empirical data that may confirm our semantic hypothesis.

4.3 *Additional Evidence for the Analysis*

We have shown that the two available readings for *laisser* are enhanced from structural constraints. The authorise interpretation is constrained by the possibility of constructing a sentence where the lower agent is interpreted also structurally as the agent of the embedded verb: in pre-v constructions, *laisser* embeds a clause whose subject is interpreted as an external argument, i.e. an agent (possibly by a VoiceP) – the embedded clause denotes then a proposition in the set of the agent's alternatives.

In Post-v constructions, on the other hand, *laisser* embeds a reduced vP, with no external argument. The interpretation is that of an event description, and not of a propositional complement qualifying as an alternative choice.

But to what extent does grammar see conceptual objects such as alternative propositions? In this section, we present a few empirical observations pointing to the conclusion that alternative propositions indeed enter the semantic component which is processed by grammar.

More specifically, following our analysis we expect at least two types of structural correlates, related to: (i) the complement of *laisser:* whether it is a propositional or a non-propositional complement; (ii) the presence vs. absence of available alternatives for the lower agent. In this section we mention two phenomena that seem to depend on a sensitivity to these two parameters.

4.3.1 Negation

The first observed empirical difference between preverbal and postverbal constructions has to do with the possibility of embedding a negative operator in the former case. Assuming that alternatives are propositional in preverbal constructions, we expect that a negative operator can apply to the complement of *laisser* in this construction. Indeed, under an authorise reading the causative verb can embed a clausal negation. Sentence (21a) is to be understood in a context where the judge authorises the defendant to answer a question; in the same courtroom situation, (21b) is perfectly acceptable if the defendant expresses the intention not to answer the question, and the judge authorises him to do so.

(21) a. La juge a laissé l'accusé répondre.
 the judge laisser.PF the-defendant answer
 'The judge let the defendant answer.'

 b. La juge a laissé l'accusé ne pas répondre.
 the judge laisser.PF the-defendant NEG answer
 'The judge let the defendant not answer.'

Conversely, we assume that event descriptions are not propositional, and therefore we expect that the complement of *laisser* cannot host a (propositional) negative operator in postverbal constructions. Thus, while (22a) is compatible with a context where the judge does not impede the defendant from answering, (22b) is ill-formed.

(22) a. La juge a laissé répondre l'accusé.
 the judge laisser.PF answer the-defendant
 'The judge let the defendant answer.'

b. *La juge a laissé ne pas répondre l'accusé.
   the judge laisser.PF NEG answer the-defendant

The ill-formedness of (22b) can be explained both on structural and semantic grounds: the syntactic constraint would say that the clausal negation *ne pas* cannot be expressed in a reduced vP structure, but one can also argue that there is no sense in which the judge could interrupt the occurrence of a non-event.

4.3.2 Agency as Choice: Defeasability of Causative Entailments and Free Choice

Recall that the main difference between preverbal and postverbal constructions concerns the possibility for the lower agent to have a choice over a set of alternatives in the former case: in preverbal constructions, the agentive subject of *laisser* allows the lower agent to keep all the alternatives in their choice set available (23).

(23) a. La juge a laissé l'accusé parler.
       the judge laisser.PF the-defendant speak
     b. Judge sets the value of $\text{ALT}_{\text{defendant}} := \{speak, not\ speak\}$

In this framework, an influence such as that exerted by the subject of the matrix verb can be conceived as guiding the *preference* for one choice among the alternative options within the set (see also section 3.2 above). The lack of constraints observed in the complement of *laisser* in (23) can then be formalised in terms of an *indifference* relation among the propositions in the ALT set (see Staraki 2017 for a formal implementation of indifference in a possible-world semantics, and Raffy 2021 for a causal model implementation). In plain words, indifference means that the two propositions p and *not-p* are not ranked in terms of preference with respect to one another, because the subject of *laisser*, who exerts the influence, chooses not to posit any ordering on them.

If we are right, we therefore expect that an indifference relation among alternatives in the complement of *laisser* may be observed only when the subject of laisser is an intentional agent, who can choose not to rank the alternatives; also, a preference choice over the alternatives is expected to depend on the ability of the lower subject, as an intentional agent, to make a choice. Next, we may also expect that the presence of an alternative set may trigger the use of lexical or functional items sensitive to semantic environments that denote choice over possible alternative worlds or propositions. In the following, we will provide two sets of empirical observations that confirm our expectations.

The first observation concerns the (non-)implicative interpretation of causal relations. We have seen in section 2.1 that Wolff & Song's (2003) taxonomy of causal categories predicts that the causative meaning of *laisser* as an ENABLE verb is non-implicative: the endstate represents a tendency, and it is envisaged once the direction of the resultant vector is defined. It "does not require that the result event occur before it can be said that causation has occurred" (Wolff & Thorstad 2016: 150), and implicative readings, by which the endstate is asserted to occur, would rely on an independent dimension, which is given in this framework by the length of the endstate vector.

This conceptual representation agrees with the observation that authorise readings of *laisser* are non-implicative, in the sense that the endstate need not be reached for the *laisser*-sentence to be felicitous. Thus, the continuation in (24b) is not considered a contradictory statement, but it may be analysed as the cancellation of an implicature arising from the expectation that Causees follow their tendency in acting.

(24) a. La   juge   a laissé   l'accusé   parler ...
        the   judge   laisser.PF the-defendant   speak ...
    b. ... mais   finalement   il   est resté   silencieux.
        but   in the end   he   stay.PF   silent
    'The judge let the defendant speak, but in the end he kept silent.'

In the framework adopted in this paper, the non-implicativity of ENABLE verbs can be translated by saying that the matrix subject of *laisser* does indeed exert an influence (therefore, causation occurs), but lower agents, despite having a tendency towards the endstate denoted by the prevalent *p*, still keep all the alternatives *p* and *not-p* in their choice set available. The defeasibility of the causative entailment for ENABLE-verbs is thus compatible with the configuration given in force theory. We take a step further in this paper and claim that there is also a grammatical dimension to this cognitive representation.

On the semantic side, the defeasibility of the entailment that the endstate has been reached is observed only when the causative relation involves two agentive participants. Thus, in sentences (25) and (26), where either one of the Causer and Causee is non-agentive, asserting that the endstate has not been reached yields a contradiction.

(25) Sa   réponse   m' a laissé   comprendre   un   certain   nombre   de
     his   answer   CL-CL-laisser.PF   understand   a   certain   number   of
     choses   #mais   finalement   je   ne   les   ai pas comprises.
     things   but   in the end   I   NEG   CL   understand.PF
     'His answer let me understand quite a few things, #but in the end I did not understand them.'

(26) Jean a laissé couler l'eau dans la baignoire
John laisser.PF flow the-water in the tub
#mais finalement l'eau n'a pas coulé.
but in the end the-water NEG flow.PF
'Jean let the water flow in the tub, #but in the end the water did not flow'

The relation between the defeasibility of causative entailments and the (agentive) properties of the subject has been already observed in the literature, where this phenomenon has received different analyses under various labels (see a.o. Martin 2015, Martin & Schäfer 2012, 2014 analysis of *non-culminating entailments* and *defeasible causative verbs*, and Copley & Harley's (2014) *defeasible causation*). Here we use the label "defeasible entailment" in a descriptive way, without strong commitment to a specific analysis; note however that the correlation between agentivity and defeasibility is expected in our framework, since only agentive subjects can choose not to impose an ordering between the alternatives. What is more interesting for our present concern is that defeasibility is also subject to a *structural* condition with *laisser*: the causative entailment appears to be non-defeasible when *laisser* embeds a vP complement in the postverbal construction, and this happens independently of the agentive potential of the lower agent. In (27), the judge can be considered, categorically speaking, an animate entity who is potentially intentional; nevertheless, contrary to (23b), the continuation in (27b) is considered degraded by most speakers.

(27) a. L'accusé a laissé parler la juge ...
the-defendant laisser.PF speak the judge
b. ??mais finalement elle est restée silencieuse.
but in the end she stay.PF silent
('The defendant let the judge speak, but in the end she kept silent.')

Once again, to our mind, the reason why the entailment is not defeasible in (27) has to do with the type of complement that *laisser* embeds in this construction. In (27), the defendant does not give the judge the choice to speak, but merely fails to prevent an event from occurring. Additionally, there is flavour that the action has already started: sentence (27a) is considered odd by native speakers in a context where an inceptive interpretation is forced on the embedded event, as in (28):

(28) La salle d'audience était silencieuse.
 The courtroom was silent.
 #Finalement, l'accusé a laissé parler la juge
 finally the-defendant laisser.PF speak the judge

Next, let's consider a further empirical fact that follows from the assumption that authorise-*laisser* involves an alternative set: only in these constructions are certain free-choice items licensed in the embedded clause. Recall that the subject of *laisser*, in virtue of her position of authority, offers a choice to the lower agent by choosing not to order the alternatives in the ALT set in terms of preference with respect to one another (an *indifference* relation).

The presence of non-ranked available alternatives seems to be relevant for licensing Free Choice Items (FCIS) like the French determiner *n'importe qu-* '(just) any', which has been described as conveying a meaning of indiscriminacy (Jayez & Tovena 2005, Vlachou 2006, 2007).

(29) Le passager a laissé le conducteur se garer à
 the passenger laisser.PF the driver park in
 n'importe quelle place pourvu qu' elle soit libre
 n'importe qu-F.SG place provided that it be.SBJ free
 'The passenger let the driver park in any place, provided it was an available one.'

According to Vlachou (2007:52) "indiscriminacy implies that an agent makes a choice in such a way that, before choosing, any alternative is equally probable to be chosen", and results in a "random selection by an agent of an entity out of a set of alternatives" (2007:131). In complex causatives, indiscriminacy would be the result of the Causer's choice to keep all alternatives equally ranked in terms of accessibility for the lower agent in the embedded clause. The fact that the lower agent does not seem to randomly choose an option would then be imputable to the meaning of *laisser*, which, as an ENABLE verb, conveys the meaning that there is a tendency of the Causee towards the prevalent p.

FCIS such as *n'importe qu-* are more generally not available in configurations where the lower agent's choice is already constrained from the causative meaning of the matrix verb, as in the case of *forcer* 'force' in (30).

(30) #Le passager a forcé le conducteur à se garer à
the passenger force.PF the driver to park in
n'importe quelle place pourvu qu' elle soit libre
n'importe quel place provided that it be.SBJ free
('The passenger forced the driver to park in any place, provided it was an available one.')

Although the issue of the licensing of FCI is a complex one, and its detailed discussion goes far beyond the scope of this paper, we believe that the contrast observed between (29) and (30) can in principle be explained by assuming that lexical causative verbs constrain the set of alternatives denoted by their complement in different ways.

5 Conclusions

An agent's actions and intentions can be furthered or hindered in multiple ways. Across languages, verbs that lexicalize causative primitives can help us understand the nature of agency and intention, precisely because they involve multiple participants which may be in a position of influencing each other via different types of force relations.

In causal relations, free choice can be restricted (or highlighted) through authority: we define authority as an agent's intrinsic ability to influence another agent's choice of action.

The goal here was to probe the relation between authority and intentional causation by looking at a construction where the causative verb expresses an ENABLE relation (Wolff and Song 2003, Wolff 2007) between agentive participants.

We have shown that authority relations are visible in grammar: authority is possible only when both participants are mapped as agents in the structure, and reversing authority relations with *laisser* is not felicitous in the cases where authority is relevant, as we have seen in the authorise scenarios with the pre-v structure for *laisser*.

Acknowledgements

We are grateful to the audience of the workshop *Agency and Intentions in Language*, where this work was first presented, for their feedback. We would like to thank in particular Julie Goncharov and Hedde Zeijstra for editing this volume, and the two anonymous reviewers for their very helpful comments. The research leading to this article has been supported by the German Research Foundation (DFG) as part of the project *Composing events in Romance causative constructions and the semantics of causation* (Project-ID 361344414) at the University of Cologne, Department of German Language und Literatur I, Linguistics.

References

Abeillé, Anne, Godard, Danièle and Miller, Philip. 1997. Les causatives en français, un cas de compétition syntaxique. *Langue française* 115: 62–74.

Alexiadou, Artemis, Anagnostopoulou, Elena, and Schäfer, Florian. 2015. *External arguments in transitivity alternations: A layering approach*, vol. 55. Oxford: Oxford University Press.

Alsina, Alex. 1992. On the argument structure of causatives. *Linguistic Inquiry* 23(4): 517–555.

Anscombe, Gertrude E. M. 1957. Intention. *Proceedings of the Aristotelian Society*. Vol. 57(1). Oxford: Oxford University Press.

Bjorkman, Bronwyn and Elizabeth Cowper. 2013. Inflectional shells and the syntax of causative *have*. *Actes du congrès annuel de l'Association Canadienne de Linguistique 2013*.

Borel, Maurice. 1972. *Sémantique des factitives en français*. MA dissertation, Université Paris 8 – Vincennes St Denis.

Copley, Bridget. 2008. The plan's the thing: Deconstructing futurate meanings. *Linguistic Inquiry* 39(2): 261–274.

Copley, Bridget. 2019. Force dynamics. In Truswell, Robert (ed.), *The Oxford handbook of event structure*, Oxford: Oxford University Press.

Copley, Bridget and Harley, Heidi. 2014. Eliminating causative entailments with the force-theoretic framework: The case of the Tohono O'odham frustrative *cem*. In Copley, Bridget and Martin, Fabienne, *Causation in Grammatical Structures*, 120–151. Oxford: Oxford University Press.

Copley, Bridget and Harley, Heidi. 2015. A force-theoretic framework for event structure. *Linguistics and Philosophy* 38(2): 103–158.

Donazzan, Marta and Lucia M. Tovena (2016) Dispositions in event nouns: decomposing the agentivity constraint. In Martin, Fabienne, Pitteroff, Marcel and Pross, Tillmann (eds.) *Morphological, syntactic and semantic aspects of dispositions*. SinSpec Series of SFB732, University of Stuttgart.

Dowty, David. 1979. *Word Meaning and Montague Grammar. The semantics of verbs and times in generative semantics and in Montague's PTQ*. Dordrecht: Reidel.

Fodor, Jerry A. 1970. Three reasons for not deriving *kill* from *cause to die*. *Linguistic Inquiry* 1(4): 429–438.

Folli, Raffaella and Harley, Heidi. 2007. Causation, obligation, and argument structure: On the nature of little v. *Linguistic Inquiry* 38(2): 197–238.

Grano, Thomas. 2017. The logic of intention reports. *Journal of Semantics* 34, 587–632.

Guasti, Maria Teresa. 1996. Semantic Restrictions in Romance Causatives and the Incorporation Approach. *Linguistic Inquiry* 27(2): 294–313.

Hale, Ken and Keyser, Samuel Jay. 1993. On argument structure and the lexical expression of syntactic relations. In Richard Kayne, Raffaella Zanuttini & Thomas Leu (eds.), *An annotated syntax reader. Lasting insights and questions*, 312–327. Chichester, UK: Wiley-Blackwell.

Harley, Heidi. 2013. External arguments and the Mirror Principle: On the distinctness of Voice and v. *Lingua* 12: 34–57.

Jayez, Jacques and Tovena, Lucia. 2005. Free choiceness and non-individuation. *Linguistics and Philosophy* 28: 1–71.

Kayne, Richard S. 1975. *French Syntax: The Transformational Cycle*. Cambridge, MA: MIT Press.

Kratzer, Angelika. 1996. Severing the external argument from its verb. In: Johan Rooryck and Laurie Zaring (eds.), *Phrase structure and the lexicon*. (Studies in Natural Language and Linguistic Theory 33), 109–137. Dordrecht: Springer.

Lauer, Sven and Prerna Nadathur. 2018. Sufficiency causatives. Ms. University of Konstanz and Stanford University.

Lauer, Sven and Prerna Nadathur. 2020. Causal necessity, causal sufficiency, and the implications of causative verbs. *Glossa* 5 (1), 49.1–37.

Mari, Alda and Fabienne Martin. 2007. Tense, abilities and actuality entailments. *Proceedings of the 16th Amsterdam Colloquium*.

Martin, Fabienne. 2015. Explaining the link between agentivity and non-culminating causation. In Sarah D'Antonio, Mary Moroney & Carol Rose Little (eds.), *Proceedings of SALT 25*, 246–266. Stanford University.

Martin, Fabienne and Schäfer, Florian. 2012. The modality of offer and other defeasable causative verbs. In Nathan Arnett & Ryan Bennett (eds.), *Proceedings of WCCFL 30*, 248–258. Somerville, MA: Cascadilla Proceedings Project.

Martin, Fabienne and Schäfer, Florian. 2014. Causation at the syntax-semantics interface. In Bridget Copley and Fabienne Martin (eds.), *Causation in grammatical structures*, 209–244. Oxford: Oxford University Press.

Neeleman, Ad and Van de Koot, Hans. 2012. The linguistic expression of causation. In Martin Everaert, Marijana Marelj & Tal Siloni (eds.), *The theta system: Argument structure at the interface*, 20–51. Oxford: Oxford University Press.

Raffy, Clémentine, 2021. Letting in Romance. Université Paris 8 and Universität zu Köln PhD thesis.

Ramchand, Gillian. 2008. *Verb meaning and the lexicon: A first-phase syntax* (Cambridge Studies in Linguistics 116). Cambridge: Cambridge University Press.

Rooth, Mats. 1992. A theory of focus interpretation. *Natural language semantics* 1(1): 75–116.

Shibatani, Masayoshi. 1976. The grammar of causative constructions: A conspectus. In Masayoshi Shibatani (ed.), *The grammar of causative constructions*, 1–40. Leiden: Brill.

Staraki, Eleni. 2017. Necessity, intention, and causation: from force interaction to eliminating the causative entailments. Draft 04.04.2017 (available at https://www.estaraki.com/research).

Talmy, Leonard. 1983. How language structures space. In Herbert L. Pick Jr. & Linda P. Acredolo (eds.), *Spatial orientation: Theory, research, and application*, 225–282. Boston, MA: Springer.

Talmy, Leonard. 1988. Force dynamics in language and cognition. *Cognitive Science* 12: 49–100.

Talmy, Leonard. 2000. *Toward a cognitive semantics: Typology and process in concept structuring*, vol. 2. Cambridge, MA: MIT Press.

Vlachou, Evangelia. 2006. Definite and indefinite free choice items: Evidence from English, Greek and French. In Pascal Denis, Brian J. Reese, Eric McCready & Alexis Palmer (eds.), *Proceedings of the 2004 Texas Linguistics Society Conference: Issues at the semantics-pragmatics interface*, 150–159. Somerville, MA: Cascadilla Proceedings Project.

Vlachou, Evangelia. 2007. *Free choice in and out of context: Semantics and distribution of French, Greek and English free choice items*. Utrecht: Utrecht University (PhD-Thesis).

Wolff, Phillip. 2003. Direct causation in the linguistic coding and individuation of causal events. *Cognition* 88: 1–48.

Wolff, Phillip. 2007. Representing causation. *Journal of Experimental Psychology: General* 136(1): 82–111.

Wolff, Phillip and Song, Grace. 2003. Models of causation and the semantics of causal verbs. *Cognitive Psychology* 47: 276–332.

Wolff, Phillip and Thorstad, Robert. 2017. Force dynamics. In Michael Waldmann (ed.), *The Oxford Handbook of Causal Reasoning*, 147–168. Oxford: Oxford University Press.

Index

ability   10, 37, 76–77, 83, 98n, 108
actuality entailment   82, 84
alternatives   96–97, 101–108
animacy   8
applicative   58, 67
aspect   30, 43, 84
attitude predicates   28–33, 38n
authority   91, 94, 95, 98, 99–101, 107

causal relations   89, 91–93, 101, 104, 108
causation by omission   101–102
causative construction   89–90, 97
causative verb   89–90, 92–94, 97, 99, 101, 108
choice   95–99, 104–105, 106–107
circumstantial modal construction   63, 68, 71, 74
CMC. *See* circumstantial modal construction
control   44, 46, 47, 96

de se   28, 29, 31–33, 39, 40, 44, 45, 49
director   37, 38, 47
doxastic predicates   28, 35–37, 40, 48, 49

embedded clause   28, 29, 32, 35n, 96, 102, 107
epistemic access   27n
epistemic predicates   48, 49
evidentiality   34, 35, 38, 42

first person   28, 32
force   91–94, 98
force variability   79–81, 83–84
futurate   37, 38, 41

indifference   104, 107
influence   90–91, 93–95, 97–99, 101–102, 104–105
intentions as force   90, 93–96, 98–99, 103, 108
introspection   9, 29n, 88, 90, 93–95, 108
involuntary agent construction   56–58, 61

modality   35, 39, 46
mood
   indicative   27, 28, 37, 43, 45, 49
   infinitive   44, 46, 47, 89, 91, 96, 102
   subjunctive   27n

oblique causer construction   58, 60, 63, 65, 71, 74
obviation   27n
OCC. *See* oblique causer construction

psych-verbs   47–49

self-knowledge   28, 33, 34, 37, 47, 48, 49
semifactive predicates   43, 44

tendency   92, 98, 101, 105
tense
   future   35, 37–39, 41
   past   30, 32, 40, 41
   present   38, 43

voice   30, 58, 59, 66, 69, 70, 72, 73, 78, 83

way-construction   2–4

www.ingramcontent.com/pod-product-compliance
Lightning Source LLC
Chambersburg PA
CBHW052051300426
44117CB00012B/2078